Congratulations on Your Graduation! But Were You Ever Educated about Life After Graduation?

What You Really Need to Know!

Lee Black

Introduction

If I could go back in time to when I graduated from high school or college, there is just one graduation gift that I really wish that someone had given to me. **It is THIS book!**

This is THE book that would have actually prepared me for life after graduation, it is about the real world, and it is filled with the ultimate truths that have taken me half a lifetime to uncover! This book is ideal for everyone. This is the final textbook that every graduate needs to ace the most important test of all, the test of life!

Students live in an artificial and unrealistic world where their success is based on memorizing and regurgitating facts and figures. Students adapt to a classroom world where they are fairly judged against others based on their memory and their ability to follow provided instructions. There usually are no work place politics or bias judgements on one's appearance and background in the classroom. Students only need to face mostly fair and objective tests. In our educational institutions there is little or no mention about how every aspect of one's appearance and background will be unfairly judged by the world that awaits them after graduation.

Students are often told how intelligent they are, but are never actually taught how to think. They solve no real life problems, but they make the Dean's list. They are not taught how to generate a creative or original thought, but get an "A" by summarizing a book created by someone else. Often students are simply told what to think from the bias perspective of their teacher and their educational institution. So when they graduate they actually have no education on how to think independently, or on how to handle their life.

When I graduated everyone told me how smart I was, and they seemed to imply that getting all those "A" grades and degrees completely prepared me for the future. But deep down inside I had so many unanswered questions, **I found out the hard way that I was completely uneducated for the rest of my life after graduation!**

Here are the unanswered life questions that I struggled with: How do you interview for a job? How do you improve your job performance? How do you deal with human bias and work place politics? How do you move up in your career? How do you start and grow your own business? How do you manage your money? How do you stay fit and healthy? How do you build strong positive relationships? How do you stay fit and healthy? And the ultimate question - How do you get more joy in life?

So now, looking back on it all, I decided to create the book that answers the questions I had when I graduated. This is THE GRADUATION BOOK and THE REST OF YOUR LIFE BOOK! The truths revealed here will entertain you and shock you! But ultimately this is THE higher education textbook that will allow you to achieve more, to have more, and to enjoy more for the rest of your life!

How to Interview for a Job

Most graduates are aware of the basic information on interviewing which we will look at next, but you were never taught the three key points which will be revealed at the end of this chapter.

First we need to be aware of the basics of handling a job interview below:

If you are expected to submit a resume, then submit one. A resume is a chance for you to list your relevant education, work experience, and skills for the job you seek. It is also a way to advertise your strengths to an employer which makes it easier for the interviewer to interview you, to recommend you to other hiring managers, and to justify hiring you. Make sure your resume highlights the reasons why you are a great candidate for the job. If you do not bother to connect the dots from you to the job you seek, then it is unlikely the interviewer will bother to hire you.

Do your research. Learn as much as you can about the company and the position you are applying for. This will show the interviewer that you are interested in the job and that you have taken the time to prepare.

Be on time. Punctuality shows that you are respectful of the interviewer's time and that you are serious about the job. An interviewer will logically assume that you will always be late to work if you can not even show up for the interview on time!

Dress professionally. First impressions matter, so make sure you dress appropriately for the interview. This doesn't mean you have to wear a suit, but you should dress in clean, neat, and professional attire.

Be polite and respectful. This means using good manners, being respectful of the interviewer's time, and avoiding negative comments about past employers or experiences. We all have negative experiences and there are many horrible employers and bosses, but you want the interviewer to think back on your interview and smile.

Be prepared to answer questions. The interviewer will likely ask you a variety of questions about your skills, experience, and why you are interested in the job. Often they will use open ended broad questions like, "Tell me about yourself?" Be prepared to answer these questions in a clear, concise, and confident manner. And figure out a way to talk about your strengths in your answers.

Ask questions. At the end of the interview, you will likely have the opportunity to ask the interviewer questions. This is your chance to learn more about the company and the position. Be sure to ask thoughtful questions that show you are interested in the job. Not asking questions will be interpreted by some interviewers as no interest or enthusiasm for the job. Remember in some ways you are also interviewing the employer to decide if they meet your standards, so ask some questions to learn about them.

Follow up. After the interview, you can send a thank-you note to the interviewer. This is a great way to reiterate your interest in the job, to thank the interviewer for their time, and to increase the chances of getting the job.

Be yourself. Don't try to be someone you're not. The interviewer will be able to tell if you're being fake, and it will hurt your chances of getting the job. Another important reason to be yourself will be mentioned a little bit later in this book.

Be positive. Smile, make eye contact, and speak in a clear and confident voice. Show the interviewer that you are excited about the job and that you would be a valuable asset to the company. If you do not show a positive interest in them and the job, they will most likely lose interest in hiring you.

Be prepared to sell yourself. The interviewer wants to know why you are the best person for the job. Be prepared to talk about your skills, experience, and why you would be a good fit for the company.

Be confident. Believe in yourself and your abilities. If you don't believe in yourself, then no one else will. This is especially true of an interviewer who has never met you.

Ok all of the information above is what most people are able to figure out with a little digging and help. Next we will look into three points about interviews we are rarely if ever taught in educational institutions or anywhere else - **the one and only interview question, the timing of your interview, and what your interview goal should be**.

The One and Only Interview Question

Every interview question is asking just one question, and when you know the question, and how to answer it, then you will nail your interviews!

Scholars, HR professionals, administrators, highly educated, and very intelligent individuals all try to create the perfect interview questions for all different types of jobs and professions. What I have figured out later in life after interviewing hundreds of candidates for different businesses and my own businesses is it is all bull…., well you know.

My experience is that most highly educated and intelligent interviewers actually have no idea how to interview or even what they are looking for. So they hide behind a bunch of confusing meaningless ineffective random questions and evaluation techniques. Some even have a long list of questions the interviewer must ask the candidate.

One of the most foolish things people do in life is make simple things complicated. I believe this actually shows one's ignorance, lack of understanding, and insecurity.

For an example of how anyone can make a simple thing complex and confusing I will use a math equation. A math equation can express the number 42 in a simple or a complex way or as in this example:

What does X mean?

"X= ((11 - 2) x (1+2)) - (12/2) + 20 + 1"

or one could simply say "**X = 42**"

Is the complex expression of the meaning of X the best way to communicate and to conduct business? Or is it just a way to look intelligent to others? The meaning of X is 42, and the meaning I am trying to convey is that in both life and in interviews - keep it simple!

I would argue that understanding how to interview simplifies the amount and type of questions that need to be asked. And this same understanding helps one in creating their interview answers.

I have found that there is only one simple question that every interviewer is attempting to ask, and it is the same question that every candidate is attempting to answer. This is because the entire purpose of an interview is about finding one thing!

So what is the one question that needs to be answered in every interview. **"Why are you the best candidate for this job?"** That is it! If the interviewer does not ask you this question in some form, then they do not know what the h… they are doing!

If the ONE question is never asked in some form during the interview, then you must work the answer to the question into your response to some other idiotic question they ask. You should always find a way to answer it at some appropriate time before the end of your interview.

You can prepare for an interview by writing down your greatest strengths and then practicing mentioning them when stating why you are the BEST candidate for a job. Then practice ways to answer those random complex foolish interview questions in a way that allows you to answer the ONE question so you can state why you are the best candidate for the job.

The Timing of Your Interview

The second thing about interviews that no educational institution prepares you for is timing. Too many people waste their time applying for jobs at the wrong time. **The timing of when you apply and interview for a job often determines if you get the job!**

What is the timing of an interview? In some ways interviewing is a numbers game. The more people applying for a job, the less likely each person is to get the job. But what if you could apply for a job before most, or even before any other candidates apply? The fact is many available jobs never get listed, or they are listed after the hiring managers have already chosen someone!

To master the interview we need to take advantage of timing because it can limit, or eliminate, all of our interview competition! For example, if a business is about to create a new position that you are interested in, by seeking out information about the position and the managers of it, you can prepare to become one of the first candidates to be interviewed. The hiring managers may even be so pleased with your initiative, your interview, and your interest that they may just hire you without ever listing the open position to anyone! And even if they do list it they may no longer give any serious consideration to anyone else. Timing allows you to eliminate most of the other hundreds of people competing for a job. In fact, your timing can be the difference between applying for a position that hundreds of people have already applied for or that is already filled, and applying for a position in which you are the one and only candidate to even be considered!

Your Interview Goal

The third point on interviews that is not taught is what your goal should be when you interview for a job. Some people would say the goal is to get the job, others would say it is to get the experience, but I would argue that neither is the answer.

For those who like the experience of interviews - I would suggest they look a little harder to find fun things to do!

And for those who measure the success of their interview by whether they get the job, I would say I used to think that way too, but I was missing something.

The truth I found is that we do not control the actions of others, and we should not let the actions of others determine how we measure our success, or how we view ourself. We could be the perfect candidate for a job, dress perfectly, answer the interview questions perfectly, and follow up perfectly; and we could still have no chance of getting the job. The employer may have already offered the job to someone but just had to list the open position; or they may be bias towards hiring a male, a female, or a person of a certain race (yes racism and bias judgements really do happen, and it can happen to anyone).

A bias interviewer may decide you are not good looking enough, or too good looking, too tall or not tall enough. They may unfairly judge you as too heavy or too thin. They may eliminate you from getting a job for reasons completely out of our control, and for reasons which are completely unfair. So whether we get the job or not is not the best measure of our interview success.

How should we measure our interview success? We can ask ourself how well we answered the one and only true interview question, and if we presented our honest self. If we tell the interviewer exactly why we feel we are the best candidate for the position (explain a few of our best traits that relate to the job), and if we are ourself (genuine or just not pretending to be something we are not); then our interview was a success!

In fact, if we are not hired it may be a good thing, not every job is for every person, and if an employer or manager does not appreciate you for who you really are then they are likely not unworthy of your time and devotion. And even if you had gotten the job, you might have had regrets and a loss of your joy working for them.

Now you have it, your education on how to interview to get the job you want! And even how to self-evaluate your interview performance.

Next we will learn how to improve the performance in each job you get.

How to Improve Your Job Performance

So you have interviewed and landed the job that you were seeking, but now what? Now you need to perform the job well. You need to know how to perform and how to improve your job performance to keep that job and to advance.

How do you improve your job performance? It starts by setting clear goals and expectations for yourself. Ask yourself what do you want to achieve in your role? Think about your manager's expectations of you as you set your goals? Once you know what you're working towards, then you can break the goal down into smaller, more manageable goals.

Plan and prioritize your work. It's important to know what needs to be done and when it needs to be done. Create a to-do list and prioritize your tasks accordingly. Working on first things first will improve your performance and your timeliness of completing tasks. Completing important tasks on time will increase your employer's confidence in you and it will also increase your chance of being promoted.

Be organized and efficient. This means having a system for keeping track of your work, managing your time effectively, and avoiding distractions. Organizing your work tasks can often increase the amount of work you accomplish in a limited time frame.

Communicate effectively. This means being clear and concise in your written and verbal communication, as well as being able to listen effectively. Communication is the key to many things, but being good at it requires several things. First we need to understand the message we are communicating and make the main points stand out in our communication. Next we need to decide the method of communication that will work best for the recipients and for your time frame and convenience. And finally we need to understand our audience. If the message one is sending is not urgent and the recipient is always busy or on the phone, it may be better to email or text the message then to spend the time trying to call when they are not busy. Or if the message is important or urgent it may be best to call the recipient. And the most important and most neglected part of good communication is just being able to shut up and **listen** to the other person!

Be a team player. This means being willing to help out your colleagues, being supportive of their work, and being able to work effectively in a group setting. This term "team player" is over used and sounds corny, but I think of it a different way. To me being a team player is just *caring about your co-workers and regularly taking voluntary actions to help them succeed.*

Be positive and enthusiastic. This will help you stay motivated and engaged in your work, and it will also make you more enjoyable to work with. Imagine how you would feel if you had to work day in and day out, week after week, month after month, and year after year with someone who complained about everything and everyone. How would you feel about coming to work, and how would you feel about that negative person? It benefits everyone to be a positive, supportive, and enthusiastic co-worker that people look forward to working with. It helps make your workplace a positive place that supports high performance and job satisfaction.

Take breaks. It's tempting to work through lunch or stay late at the office, but taking breaks is essential for productivity. Get up and move around, or step outside for some fresh air. Regular breaks where you move around will improve both your health and your performance.

Delegate tasks. If you have too much on your plate, don't be afraid to delegate tasks to others. This will free up your time so you can focus on the most important things. Do not let ego or lack of trust prevent you from delegating some tasks, delegating is an effective tool for getting things done and an essential tool for managers.

Ask for help. If you're struggling with a task, don't be afraid to ask for help from your manager or colleagues. They may be able to offer you some guidance or resources. Again you have to step away from ego and understand that no one knows everything about everything. Asking for help is not a weakness, it is a strength, a strength that allows one to do more, and to do it better.

Take care of yourself. Make sure you're getting enough sleep, eating healthy foods, and exercising regularly. Taking care of your physical and mental health will help you perform your best at work.

Continue to learn about the job. A specific thing you can do to improve your performance in your specific role is to strive to become more knowledgeable about the job. For example, if you're an automobile mechanic you could focus on learning the most advanced and efficient repair methods for the cars you work on. Or, if you're a salesperson, you could work on developing your sales network and learning new ways to efficiently advertise to customers.

The most important thing is to be proactive and intentional about your job performance. Do not expect or wait for your employer or manager to do anything for you. Set goals, track your progress, and seek feedback from others. With a little time and consistent effort, you can improve your performance and reach your full potential in your job.

How to Deal with Workplace Politics & Bias

Now you nailed your interview, got the job you wanted, and improved your job performance; but now life hits you with something unexpected and ugly. Something that your education did not prepare you to handle, workplace politics and bias!

Workplace Politics

I do not remember an any classes called workplace politics 101. Perhaps no such thing exists? Spoiler alert, workplace politics exist virtually everywhere, it affects virtually everything, and it is almost always completely unfair! So how does one deal with this?

The key to handling many unfair and ugly things in life lies in how we choose to respond to it - we can let it control us and drag us down into a negative sad place, or we can take control of it in a positive way.

Now let's look at some ways to start dealing with workplace politics in a positive and productive way:

Understand the informal network. In addition to the formal organizational chart, there is also an informal network of relationships that exists in most workplaces. And an informal network that manages things based on its own interests. This network can be a powerful tool for getting things done, but it can also be used for negative purposes. So by understanding who the key players are in the informal network and their interests, you can position yourself to be more effective in fitting into your work and getting things done.

Build positive relationships. The old saying that "you're only as good as your network" is especially true in the workplace. By building positive relationships with your colleagues, you create a foundation of trust and support that can help you navigate the political waters.

Be professional at all times. Even if you're dealing with people who are playing dirty, it's important to stay professional at all times. This means avoiding gossip, spreading rumors, and taking sides in conflicts. Once people understand that you will not gossip about them or betray their trust in you, then your co-workers will trust you more and they will become more loyal to you.

Speak up for yourself. If you feel like you're being treated unfairly or your ideas are being dismissed, don't be afraid to speak up for yourself. Be clear and direct about your concerns, and be prepared to back them up with evidence. It may be very uncomfortable to speak up when you feel something is unfair, but it is a worse feeling to do nothing knowing your silence condones and perpetuates unfairness in the workplace.

Don't take it personally. It's easy to get caught up in the emotional side of workplace politics, but it's important to remember that it's often not personal. People may be acting out of their own self-interest, or they may simply be misinformed. Try to stay objective and focus on the facts. We have no control over the bad things that others decide to do, but we do not have to let their actions control our actions and emotions, or even let them drag us down into the mud with them.

Be aware of your own biases. We all have our own biases, and these can sometimes cloud our judgment when it comes to workplace politics. Be aware of your own biases and try to be objective in your dealings with others.

Remember that you're not alone. Workplace politics can be tough, but you do not have to face it alone. Many people have to deal with these issues on a daily basis. There are resources where you can find support from others, and even from those who are going through the same thing. Having a workplace friend to confide in can make all the difference in the world!

Don't be afraid to seek help. If you're struggling to deal with workplace politics, don't be afraid to ask for help especially when something occurs that hurts you, or someone else. You can seek help from a trusted colleague, a mentor, a trustworthy manager or HR professional. You may not be able to fix everything or change everyone, but taking action and seeking help will make you feel better, and it will give your workplace some hope for change.

Workplace Bias

Even more prevalent and ugly then workplace politics is workplace bias. Human bias leads to all manners of discrimination and mistreatment of others! But how do we deal with workplace bias?

Workplace bias is a complex issue, but there are a number of things that can be done to address it. Let's look at some ways we can address workplace bias:

First be aware of your own biases. The first step to dealing with workplace bias is to be aware of your own biases. We all have biases, but it's important to be aware of them so that we can try to overcome them.

Challenge your own assumptions. When you're making decisions about people, take a moment to challenge your own assumptions. Are you making assumptions based on someone's race, gender, age, or other protected characteristic? If so, take a step back and try to see the situation from a different perspective. **Just imagine a person with the opposite characteristics doing the same thing, and ask yourself would you still judge them the same way?**

Be open to different perspectives. One of the best ways to deal with workplace bias is to be open to different perspectives. When you're working with people from different backgrounds, be willing to listen to their experiences and perspectives. This will help you to understand their point of view and to see the world from a different perspective.

Speak up against bias. If you see or experience workplace bias, don't be afraid to speak up. This doesn't mean that you have to be confrontational, but you can simply point out the bias and ask for it to be addressed.

Support policies and procedures that promote equity. If your workplace has policies and procedures in place that promote equity, support them. This could include things like unconscious bias training, diversity and inclusion initiatives, or a zero-tolerance policy for discrimination. Educate yourself about bias. There are many resources available to help you learn more about bias, such as books, articles, and online courses.

Talk to your colleagues about bias. Start a conversation with your colleagues about bias and how it can impact the workplace.

Support organizations that are working to address bias. There are many organizations that are working to address bias in the workplace. You can support their work by donating your time or money.

By taking these steps, you can help yourself and you can also help to create a workplace where everyone feels welcome and respected.

How to Move Up in Your Career

So you have mastered your job and continue to improve your job performance, you even have learned how to deal with workplace politics and bias. But now you are wondering how do you advance your career?

There are many things you can do to advance in your chosen career. Let's look at some of the best ways next:

Set clear goals. What do you want to achieve in your career? Once you know what you want, you can start to make a plan to get there. Too many people want to advance but when management asks them what they want to do and the job the wish to advance to, they say, "I don't know." The truth that no one teaches you is that if you don't take the time and the effort to decide where you want to go, then no one can help you get there!

Identify your strengths and weaknesses. What are you good at? What do you need to improve on? Once you know your strengths and weaknesses, you can start to focus on developing your skills. And this knowledge of your strengths will help you make the decision about where you want to advance to.

Get training and education. The best way to advance in your career is to keep learning. Take courses, attend conferences, and read books and articles about your field. The key to advancing in a career and getting a raise in income is to make yourself more valuable to your employer by knowing more about the business!

Network with people in your field. Get to know people who work in your industry and build relationships with them. This will help you to learn about opportunities and to get your foot in the door. Often someone in your network will alert you to new jobs or recommend you to a hiring manager.

Be proactive. Don't wait for opportunities to come to you. Be proactive and look for ways to advance your career. This could mean taking on new projects, volunteering for extra work, or speaking up in meetings. Some people even seek out a business need and figure how they can fill it by having management create a new job just for them! Don't be invisible to upper management, participate in meetings so people remember you and your name. **You can build up your advancement opportunities by building up your reputation!**

Be patient. It takes time to advance in your career. Don't get discouraged if you don't see results immediately. Just keep working hard and you will eventually reach your goals. Too many people get discouraged because they compare themselves and their progress to anyone who gets promoted i the entire company, even though they have no idea how many times that person has tried and failed or how long they have waited. It is not a race or a competition, it is just about improving yourself and creating opportunity for your own advancement. **It is foolish to compare yourself with others, this gives your power to others and to fate, but you retain your power to advance when you only focus on your accomplishments and the positive things you can do to advance.**

Be willing to take risks. If you want to advance in your career, you need to be willing to take risks. This could mean taking on new challenges, speaking up in meetings, or even asking for a specific promotion. Taking risks sometimes means looking for a job in another business or location, or taking on a new career all together.

Be persistent. Don't give up on your dreams. If you want to advance in your career, you need to be persistent and keep working hard. Not every attempt to advance will work, in fact most may fail. But **it is impossible for you to fail if you never give up!**

Be positive. A positive attitude will help you to stay motivated and to achieve your goals. It will also make you more attractive to those who can help you advance. Many people were promoted after failing the first attempt but then they chose to positively work with the hiring managers on ways to improve their chances of getting the next promotion. Positivity is noticed by everyone, and over time is will usually be rewarded!

How to Start & Grow Your Own Business

Now we know how to interview and how to work for someone else, but what about those graduates that want to start their own business?

Owning your own business may mean taking greater risks and having to think independently and creatively, but it also means that if you succeed you will probably have more freedom and make more money then you would have made working for someone else. So for those interested in this type of opportunity, this chapter is for you!

Let's look into the secrets to starting your own business that most of us were never taught in school, and then we will look at some efficient ways to grow that business.

Ultimately a business is not simply about making money, it is about filling a need or a desire of your customers. If someone just opens a business to make money then they are setting themselves up to fail. Why do I say that? The reason is a business is a two sided equation and only exists over time when both sides are satisfied. If you don't care about your customers then eventually they will find out and leave you. And they will tell many other potential customers to stay away too!

How to Start Your Own Business

Any huge task becomes easier to achieve when we can break it down into smaller tasks, or steps. So to start your own business here are the steps you can follow:

The first step is to come up with a business idea. What are you passionate about? What skills do you have? What problems can you solve for others? Once you have a general idea of what you want to do, you can start to narrow it down and develop a more concrete business plan.

The second step is to do your research. Before you launch your business, it's important to understand the market you're entering, so ask yourself some questions: Who are your target customers? What are their needs and wants? What are your competitors doing? What is the average return on investment for the type of business you plan to open? And how long does this type of business normally takes to become profitable?

The third step is to create a business plan. A business plan is a roadmap for your business. It should outline your goals, strategies, and financial projections. It's a great way to communicate your business to potential investors or partners. How do you create a great business plan? **Just think about how your business plan would make you feel if someone else presented it to you.**

The fourth step is to get funding. Unless you're lucky enough to have the money to start your business on your own, you'll need to find a way to finance it. There are a number of different ways to get funding, including loans, grants, and crowdfunding. If you have created a compelling business plan, then it will be a useful tool in getting a loan, or investors, or business partners.

Step five is choosing a business structure. There are a number of different business structures to choose from, including a sole proprietorship, partnership, LLC, and corporation. The structure you choose will have implications for your taxes, liability, and other aspects of your business. So seek help if you need it to set up the right business type.

The sixth step is to look at complying with the laws for your business and its location. Get the necessary permits and licenses. Depending on the type of business you're starting, you may need to obtain certain permits and licenses. This can vary from location to location, state to state, or country to country, so it's important to do your research.

The seventh step is to set up your business. This includes things like finding a location, getting a business bank account, and setting up your accounting system.

Here are some things to focus on when your business is up and running:

Set clear goals and objectives. What do you want to achieve with your business? Once you know your goals, you can develop a plan to achieve them.

Create a budget and track your expenses. This will help you stay on track financially and make sure you're not overspending. Plan on reinvesting a certain percentage of sales back into the business and to cover expenses before taking out money for yourself.

Delegate tasks to others. As your business grows, you won't be able to do everything yourself. Delegate tasks to others so you can focus on the most important things.

Once your business is open you have most likely done the hardest part, but there is still the challenge of growing your business.

Next we will look at what is needed to grow your business.

How Do You Grow Your Business?

There are many ways to grow a business. Each business owner needs to use what works for their business, situation, and personality. Here are some of the most effective ways to grow your business:

Focus on your customers. The best way to grow your business is to focus on your customers and their needs. What are they looking for? What problems are they trying to solve? **Once you understand your customers, you can tailor your products or services to meet their needs.**

Provide excellent customer service. This is essential for any business, but it's especially important for small businesses that are trying to compete with larger companies. *Make sure your customers are happy and they'll keep coming back for more.*

Invest in marketing and advertising. You need to let people know about your business if you want them to buy from you. Invest in marketing and advertising to reach your target audience.

Expand your product or service offerings. If you're only offering one product or service, you're limiting your potential growth. Consider expanding your offerings to reach a wider audience. For example, a person may have a store that sells only hats. But they may be able to significantly increase their total sales by adding other clothing items like shoes, belts, and clothes that go with their hats.

Partner with other businesses. Partnering with other businesses can help you reach new customers and grow your business. Look for businesses that complement your own and offer a mutually beneficial partnership. An example is a person who sells art in a retail setting may partner with different stores in the area to have them give out coupons to their store at the same time the other businesses ring up a sale.

Attend industry events. This is a great way to network with potential customers and partners. You can also learn about new trends and opportunities in your industry.

Stay up-to-date on the latest technology. Technology can help you grow your business in a number of ways. Use technology to automate tasks, improve customer service, and to reach new customers.

Be willing to change and adapt. The business world is constantly changing, so you need to be willing to change and adapt your business as well.

Don't be afraid to fail. Failure is a part of the entrepreneurial journey. The important thing is to learn from your mistakes and keep moving forward!

Find a mentor or business advisor. Having someone who has been there and done that can be invaluable. They can offer guidance and support, and they can help you avoid making costly mistakes.

Be patient and persistent. Growing a business takes time and effort. Don't get discouraged if you don't see results overnight. Keep working hard and eventually you can achieve your goals.

Don't give up. Starting a business, and growing it, is usually hard work; but it is also incredibly rewarding. If you're passionate about your business and you're willing to put in the effort, you can achieve your goals.

We have discussed working for someone else and starting a business, but we still are missing something that is extremely important to our financial future. We next will learn how to manage the money we earn in our job or business.

How to Manage Your Money

In school I learned math, how to count money, and even some of the accounting methods businesses use; but I never learned what I really needed to know in order to thrive in life. I never learned how to manage my money, or how to become wealthy. Your life is about to change when you read this chapter and take action, even if you are poor you can quickly become quite wealthy, and if you are already rich, you can become much richer.

The secrets to acquiring and managing money begins with understanding exactly what money is so that we will not be among those who are reluctant to accumulate it, and so we can better control it. Money's power comes from everyone's belief about it, we all accept and believe in it's value, and this shared belief allows it to be used to acquire other things of value. Money, or wealth, is neither good nor evil; money is simply a tool to make things happen, but it can be used for good or evil purposes.

Money simply allows one to better express who they are, whether they want to do good things, or they choose to do bad things. We all need things that cost money, so to get the most out of life we need to get control over our finances. Knowing how to acquire and grow our money gives us the power to get, and to enjoy, the things that we want for ourself and others.

The information to follow is designed to significantly multiply the total amount of money the reader will have to enjoy in their lifetime.

We will start with the simple well known ways to manage and multiply money, and then move to the more complex less known ways. We will focus on the following:

1) How to Create and Follow a Budget

2) How to Make More Money for Your Time

3) How to earn more profits with your money

How to Create and Follow a Budget

The beginning of taking control of one's financial future actually lies in restraint. Restraint is not seeking immediate gratification, it means not spending all of the money one makes as soon as they make it, or even before they make it. Restraint gives one the ability to save and to invest. And once one can save money, they can use that money in ways that will allow them to build wealth even faster.

This simple principle of financial restraint, is for many the biggest barrier to becoming wealthy. Most people can not resist the urge to spend all the money they make as soon as they make it. But the truth is that if we save and invest now, we will actually have more money to spend during our entire lifetime! And as we will see, the harder our saved money works for us, the less we will have to work for our money.

A visual example of someone trying to attain wealth can be a man trying to fill up a swimming pool with water. The water represents money, and a full pool of water represents the wealth needed to not have to work for a living. Our ability to earn money and to save a portion of it determines the size of the bucket we can use to fill up the savings swimming pool. The goal is to fill up the empty money swimming pool using buckets of water scooped up from a nearby river, called the Opportunity River. Someone who is unable to save money is like a man with a hole in his bucket. Each time he scoops up a bucket of water (money), it drips out through the hole in the bucket before he can pour it into the money savings pool. So no matter how hard he works he always has nothing.

Giving away all our money may seem like a good and a noble idea to some, but if we have no limit to the amount we give away then this is like having a money savings pool with a hole in the bottom of it. Even if our savings bucket has no hole in it, as soon as we pour from our savings bucket into our money savings pool, everything is drained away. This will aways leave us working hard and living in the stressful paycheck to paycheck zone, with an empty money savings pool.

But how do we plug up the holes in our money savings bucket and seal any leaks in our money savings pool?

The way to seal the leaks in both our money savings bucket and our money savings pool is to use a budget. **When we have a budget our money will finally stop slipping through our hands** because our money bucket will have no holes in it. And our money savings pool will have no leaks in it, and thus it will finally start to fill up.

The first secret to managing money and to creating wealth is to start saving by creating a budget that is realistic for our circumstances and that is specific to our spending habits. But how does a successful budget work, and how can we create our own budget?

A successful budget is time based and specific to our situation. In an effective budget, we actually set aside money for daily expenses, we include money to spend on a whim, and also include money to give away to others. We may even budget for unexpected expenses. Most people fail at creating an effective budget simply because they leave out personal spending money, and then they eventually splurge on things that reck their savings budget. Others forget to budget for predictable yet unexpected expenses, like car and home repairs. Everyone knows that cars eventually break down and that homes continually need repairs, but many do not budget for it, and they always seem to be hit unexpectedly whenever they have to maintain or repair something that will inevitably need continuing repairs over time. But when our budget is realistic and includes money for impulse spending and predictable unexpected expenses, then it becomes much easier to follow because of less financial surprises, and this certainty makes it easier for us to succeed at saving.

The key to a budget is to understand how much money we actually make in a period of time, and how much we normally spend in that same period of time. Many people look at a prior month to see their expenses, and the last month's pay. Then they make a list of required expenses and discretionary expenses. For example, if someone brings home $5000.00 a month after taxes and their rent/mortgage, utilities, electricity, gas, trash, water, internet, cell phone, car insurance, and car payment are all considered required expenses that add up to $3000, then $2000 is their discretionary spending. That same person may re-evaluate the money in their discretionary spending budget and determine they need at least another $600.00 for groceries, and another $300.00 for predictable yet unexpected expenses and repairs of their home and car. Then they are left with $1100.00 of discretionary funds. They could decide they want to save $600.00 a month, and they can spend $500.00 per month for impulse items, or to give some away, and/or to use some toward random entertainment. For this budget a total of $900.00 a month goes into savings,

$300.00 a month is held in savings for unexpected expenses, $600.00 a month in savings is dedicated to savings and not removed. And $500.00 is taken out in cash for impulsive spending, entertainment, and/or for giving away to others. A budget like this that specifically includes impulse money, as well as savings only money, is easier to maintain which also makes it easier for one to succeed in the long run.

Another way we can improve the odds of successfully using a budget is by making it efficient and convenient. When one saves immediately as soon as they earn money, such as having a certain amount automatically deposited into their savings from their paycheck or payroll bank account, then they are not tempted to spend the money outside of their budget. An automatic deposits directly from a person's pay as soon as they are paid increases their ability to consistently save.

The weakness of many budgets is that they do not account for impulsive spending. If we give no consideration or allocation of money to spend on whatever we desire in the moment then we leave the door open to savings failure. But when someone has money set aside for impulsive spending, for things like entertainment and giving to others, then they open the door to successful saving. The same person in the budget example above has the $500 a month cash which they can spend immediately, or save a few months to go on vacation or to buy something more expensive, or they may give away the money to others, or they may buy things for others; and all the while they are increasing their savings each month by simply following their budget. A budget allows us to cut through the greatest barrier to wealth - saving money. And as we shall see, having some savings opens the door to being able to do other things that can increase our wealth much more rapidly.

Many people believe they have a good excuse for not saving, the excuse most people give revolves around not having enough income after expenses to save. But with a little effort and creativity this excuse can almost always be overcome.

Even if a person's income currently equals their expenses and they do not wish to do any additional work to increase their income, then there are still options to save. One can look for opportunities to decrease the cost of the things they normally buy. Someone can start using coupons for food and other expenses, and then put the money saved by using coupons into their savings, then abracadabra - suddenly they can save. If another person buys their household items in bulk they can save on their overall monthly expenses and start saving that money. Yet another person may find government assistance for their food or housing expenses because of their low income, again allowing them to save a little money each month. Others may find ways to save money on their electric or gas bills by opening the shades in the winter to let the sun warm their home, or by closing the shades in the summer to keep the home cool so they use less electricity or gas. Others may carpool to work to save on gas, or to receive extra pay from their employer's carpool incentive program. Someone else may call their internet, or cell phone provider, to negotiate a lower rate on services, or they may change their service altogether and then apply the savings to their savings. Others may change the date of their seasonal vacation or travel away from holidays and weekends so they can take advantage of much lower flight and hotel rates. Others may recycle items they once threw away for extra money. Others may simply shop around to buy household items and food that they regularly buy each week from different stores at lower prices, and again take the money saved and put it into their savings. Others that drive a lot, may trade in a high priced gas guzzling truck or car, for a lower priced economic and fuel efficient vehicle, and then put the money saved on gas and car payments into savings. So even if one's income stays the same, they can still save by finding ways to cut their expenses. Regardless of your situation, if you look for it, then ways to save will appear for you too.

As we will see, if we are willing to seek ways to increasing our income, then this can also increase our ability to save. Saving is the first step towards becoming wealthy, now let's look at the next step, increasing our income.

How to Make More Money for Your Time

There are many ways to increase our income, one effective way is to simply get paid more money for our time. The secret to doing this is not really taught in schools or universities. **The secret to increasing your income is changing your perspective on what you can do and on the opportunity that exists around you.**

Here is a story that illustrates how someone can greatly increase their income based on changing their narrow perspective on the opportunities available to them and on their own abilities. This story is about a man who decided to broaden his search for opportunity beyond his dead end job, beyond his old company, and even beyond his current occupation. We get to see how a plan and person's beliefs can shape their life in a story called Job Freedom.

Job Freedom

Job is a young man working as a janitor in a small town family owned company called Clean Lamp, and he is making an hourly wage that was just above the minimum allowed wage of the land. Job is a loyal and faithful company man, and year after year he tries his best every day to meet the company standards. Job goes to his boss each year and asks for a raise, but his boss, the owner's son named Trap, says the company can't afford to pay more for his performance rating, and then just gives Job a two percent raise for the entire year, which corresponds with a good 4 star rated performance.

Each year Job does all he can to get the highest 5 star evaluation from his boss so that he can get a 3% raise. But each year Job gets the good 4 star evaluation, and he is told no one gets the higher evaluation unless they do something truly exceptional which causes the company to get a 5 star overall rating from the customers.

Job wonders what exactly is the "exceptional" perfect performance that is expected of him to get the higher raise? Job never gets a clear explanation of what he can do to get the higher raise from Trap, his Supervisor. Job suspects there is nothing he can do in his job to achieve a 5 star rating, and no one, including the managers in the same janitor position, have ever gotten the 5 star rating. Job and the other janitors working there feel that having the unrealistic 5 star evaluation on the performance evaluation is like getting a slap in the face from Clean Lamp management every time they are evaluated. But few say anything as they are all afraid to anger the managers who they feel care very little about fairness or their employees well-being.

Job's company was like many businesses, and many business managers who have no idea how to run a business or how to manage employees, but only really know how to kiss up to their manager to keep their job. Clean Lamp managers set unrealistic expectations with vague guidance of the performance they want from the employees.

Their out of touch goals and confusing guidance frustrate employees, instead of inspiring them. The managers of Clean Lamp have the information they need to improve the business in their surveys of customer satisfaction, but they do nothing constructive with it. Instead the managers continually meet with each other just to discuss the same financial statistics and data every week. The main focus of the managers is patting themselves on the back for manipulating data to make it look like they did something good, and generating reports to impress each other. And like many businesses, even if half of the managers in Clean Lamp were fired, it would have with no effect on the productivity or sales of the business, in fact it would only increase the business profits.

In the case of the Clean Lamp, the real reason the company was getting a 4 star overall evaluation, instead of a 5 star overall evaluation, was simply because the customers were having difficulty reaching the management of Clean Lamp by phone whenever they needed to change their cleaning schedule. The survey actually gave the individual janitors 5 stars on their work, but the overall company rating of 4 stars was based on things the management failed to do. In order to get the 5 star rating management should have simply changed their own policy so that they would answer their phone calls promptly, and so they would return missed calls and messages promptly.

But instead of doing their job better, each year the managers of Clean Lamp decide to blame the people they supervise for the company shortcomings. They react to the customer survey by adding the requirement of a perfect evaluation of the company by its customers, to the individual evaluation of each janitor. In other words they are evaluating their employees on something they have no control over. So each year the performance evaluation only lowers the moral of all of the employees. Yet each year Job's supervisor, Trap, pats himself on the back, just like the other managers, for having this unattainable and unrealistic standard. These incompetent managers think that it inspires the employees when they set unrealistic goals with no specific guidance on how to *reach the goal. But in reality they are just trying to hide their own incompetence at managing the business from the owner by blaming the ones they manage.*

Job sees what is happening, and he finally starts to become totally fed up. Job is fed up with doing his best in a job for an employer who is lacking recognition, with management who scapegoats the employees, with having no real promotion potential, and with having no substantial raises year after year. Job thinks about all the years that he has only received small raises, and he feels continually belittled and mocked by management too. Job feels like salt is being thrown into his wound because he knows that he does his job better then anyone else, even his customers say this in their evaluation of HIS work as a janitor.

Job's faith causes him to suffer more then most year after year. Job is a loyal hard working employee, and he has faith in what many have faith in. Job believes that all you need is "hard work" to get ahead. Because of his faith in "hard work", Job endures and suffers in the same job year after year.

*Job does not know what to do, and he even becomes emotionally down and starts to question his beliefs. Job had developed his faith in hard work based on what his father had told him as a child. Job strongly believes what many poor people believe, and what his father had told him, - **"If you work hard, then you will be rewarded and you will get ahead."***

Job suffered through several more frustrating years, but nothing changes. The company did not change, the supervisor did not change, and Job's small paycheck did not change. Then one year his wife becomes pregnant, and he finds this out a few days before his next annual company performance evaluation.

Job again asks for a 3% raise, he points out the high evaluation for his work by the customers and tells Trap that his wife is expecting, but Trap smiles and says, "It is clearly stated on the yearly performance evaluation that BOTH you and the company must receive an overall 5 star rating by customers in order for you to get an individual 5 star performance rating and raise. And you signed this goal a year ago, agreeing to it." Trap points to Job's required signature on a document last year, and smiles with great satisfaction. Trap then only gives out the usual 2% raise for a 4 star evaluation.

At the end of the work day right after Job's evaluation he goes to a bar to get a drink, and to try to forget his frustrations. On the way to the bar he stops a moment and begins to think out loud, "Hard Work, why have you forsaken me!" Later that evening as Job is sitting at the bar trying to drink his frustrations away and wishing for something better, an old man named Roy, strolls up and sits next to him. Roy notices that Job looks down. Roy then says, "How are you doing young fella, are you ok?"

Job begins telling Roy what has been happening to him each year at work. Job also tells Roy that he is even more frustrated this year with his tiny raise because his wife is pregnant and he is concerned about the rising cost of living for his growing family. Job continues to tell Roy the details about the ridiculous expectations his boss has for him to get even a tiny 3% raise, and about the unrealistic requirement for a 5 star company performance evaluation. Job tells Roy that he does his job better then anyone else, but he has never received the excellent 5 star evaluation, and neither has any other janitor. Job tells Roy how he wishes he could escape Clean Lamp so he could make a better living to support his growing family.

Roy listens to everything, and says nothing at first. Roy thinks for a moment about what he has heard, then Roy finishes his drink and looks Job in the eyes with a serious stare, and after a moment of complete silent he says,

"Your life is what you make it. Working hard at the same job for the same supervisor, and in the same business will yield you the same results.

There is a popular false belief that traps many people in a job. The false belief is that "hard work" alone will change your life. How many hard working people do you know that are broke and frustrated?

The truth is that hard work is only part of what is needed to get ahead. **The power to change one's life comes from hard work, and a plan that is based on the right knowledge.**

Why are you letting someone else decide your path and limit your future? The power to shape your future lies within you, the more power you continue to give to your supervisor and to your company, the less power is left for you to change your life. Stop looking to those outside of you to change your life and start looking within yourself. You have the power to change your life, and you even have the power to grant your wish."

After this conversation with Roy, Job stops and really begins to think, and at that moment Job finally decides he needs to take action this day and actually make a plan to change things. He asks the bar tender to buy another drink for his new friend Roy, but strangely enough the bartender says, "For who?" Job looks over and sees the empty chair next to him where Roy had been sitting, but now Roy is nowhere to be seen.

The next day Job wakes up to a sunny day with a smile on his face. Job now has a plan to finally escape Clean Lamp by making a broader search for opportunities. Job decides to look beyond his current employer and his current Supervisor, he looks beyond his current location, and even beyond his current occupation.

Job's broader search for opportunity opens the door to a better career for Job. Job's second job pays more, it is a bigger business with more upward mobility. Next Job decides to start his own cleaning business as soon as he has saved some money. With his higher income, Job finds it easier to save money with his budget, and he uses his savings to buy the equipment and the vehicle he needs to start his own cleaning service. Job starts working part time at developing his new business, while working his second job. And soon he has enough customers to only work for himself at his business. Job now can work a few hours a day at a couple of businesses making much more per hour then he did working at his first or second job.

Next Job decides to take on more business, and then he decides to hire a couple of people to help him do the work. Job reinvests his profits to buy another vehicle for his employees. Within a year, Job has multiple employees and vehicles, and he now owns a business that provides cleaning services for multiple businesses. Now Job sees that with the same amount of time invested in his first job, he makes over 10 times as much money, and he now has the freedom and flexibility to work when he wants to.

Job learns how to treat his employees from his bad experience at his old job. Job sets realistic goals for his employees that actually pertain to the job they do, which encourages his employees. He actually reads customer surveys and makes adjustments to his business based on their feedback. And his yearly evaluations are clear, specific, and realistic because they are based on things he himself can do in the same position. Job promptly responds to his customers when they call, and he never blames his employees for management shortcomings. Job's *customers rate his overall business at the highest 5 stars rating in the same survey that his old employer got the lower 4 stars evaluation. Job's business continues to rapidly grow, and it becomes even larger then Clean Lamp in the following years. And because of his commitment to fairness and respect for his employees, his employees feel inspired and appreciated which makes them thrive too.*

Job's inner genie was finally released and freed from the Clean Lamp, a business he had been trapped in for years. Job now realizes that he gave himself freedom from his old job's tiny annual raises, from his old supervisor Trap, from his old unattainable discouraging annual evaluations, and from his old lousy paycheck. Job had also freed his growing family from the clutches of poverty. Job was willing to take on new responsibilities and to look for opportunities everywhere, thus his new perspective allowed him to escape being trapped in his old job that was going nowhere.

Exactly one year after meeting Roy, Job went to celebrate his success in the same bar he met Roy at earlier. To Job's surprise, Roy walked in and again sat right next to him. Job smiled and said, "I am so glad to see you again, I just wanted to thank you! Right about now I would be trapped in my old job, I would be begging Trap for a 3% raise just to make just a little over minimum wage, and I would be getting slapped in the face by an impossible standard leading to a 2% raise. But now I work less hours, and still make way over 10 times as much money as I did a year ago! The power to change my life was within me all along, I just needed to meet someone who was wise enough to see it, and that was empathetic enough to say the words I needed to hear to release me from the Clean Lamp, a place where I had sentenced myself to be trapped in for years. What you said was all I needed to finally make a plan and to take a chance on trying something new. You inspired me to release the power that has been trapped within me for years, and it has changed my life. Now I have gotten my wish for financial freedom, I have escaped from my old supervisor Trap, and I am forever released from having to return to the Clean Lamp!"

Like the story of Job Freedom illustrates there are many ways to increase our income for our time working. And it all start within our own mind. If we can open our mind and see our full potential and all the potential that is all around us, then we increase our potential to increase our income.

Ok now that we have discussed multiple ways to increase our income, we still need to know how to manage the money we have coming in. Now we will look at how to manage and multiply the money we make.

How to earn more profits with your money

Schools and universities neglect teaching one thing that is so critical to life, they do not teach us how to invest our money! I had to learn the hard way, like so many people.

For investors it is always recommended to get advice from a licensed financial advisor, especially if someone is new at investing in stocks or other securities.

How to invest money is something that I had no idea about when I graduated, but after losing money in investments I vowed to become one of the greatest investors to ever walk the earth! And I began researching what actually works for the next couple decades.

So what secrets to investing have I learned from decades of research and experience? The key to investing is to get the best return on your assets and money for the time that it is invested, while also limiting the overall risk of potential loss.

To me investing is similar to gambling, but **true investing is gambling where the odds are always in your favor**. Professional gamblers know that not every bet will win, and professional investors know that not every investment will make a profit. But successful gambling and investing happens over time when with the odds are in your favor. When we invest in multiple investments where the odds are in our favor, then we create the environment where our money can multiply safely.

The first secret of investing is that success and failure are two sides of the same money coin. In other words, occasional losses are a normal part of successful investing.

I mastered profits and got my Doctorate Degree in investing when I created my three golden rules of investing. The rules I will reveal next are a solid gold treasure when it comes to building wealth!

Golden Rules of Investing

1. Only invest when you can accurately estimate both the chance of a potential loss and the chance of a potential profit

2. Only invest when your overall chance of profit is greater then your overall chance of loss over the long term

3. Only invest an amount you can afford to lose multiple times before you make a profit in any one single risky investment

Next is a story to illustrate how important all three rules are to gaining and maintaining wealth, and it reveals a universal principle that is the same in investing as in gambling.

Sometimes You Lose

Chance is a gambler in Las Vegas who had just lost all of his money on his birthday which is on October the 5th. Chance was sitting next to the roulette wheel with a sad and lonely look on his face. At the same time the wealthy casino owner, named Frank, saw Chance looking sad, and he also heard from his staff that he had lost all of his money on his birthday. Frank was feeling generous this day and he wanted to help Chance, and he also wanted to create an exciting event in his casino that day. So Frank sat next to Chance, and told him he was going to put the odds of winning in his favor. Frank told Chance, "I was not always wealthy and I have had my share of losing at the casinos, but one day when I was down on my luck and wishing for something better, an old man stood next to me in the casino, he listened to my story and to what I wished that I could do, and then he encouraged me to pursue my wish to go into entertainment. Once I did this my luck really changed, and now I own this entire casino."

Frank then pulled a table dealer and a gambling table to an open space in the center of the casino just for Chance. Frank told Chance he has a six sided dice, and the casino will pay out equal to the bet if the dice lands on 1,2,3, or 4; but Chance will lose the money bet if a 5 or 6 is rolled. Frank gives him $250 and says, "Since you were born today, October the fifth (10/5), I am going to give you the chance to win an amount equal to the number 10 followed by 5 zeros, or $1,000,000! Enjoy the odds in your favor for up to $1,000,000, and make sure to do it your way."

Chance is overjoyed that he now has $250 and can gamble with the odds in his favor to win as much as $1000,000! A crowd gathers around this special table set up just for Chance. And now that the odds are definitely in his favor, Chance is very excited and thinks that his luck must finally be changing. So he decides to bet the full $250 and rolls the dice. The first roll lands on a 3, so he wins, and now has $500. Chance decides to bet it all again on the second bet, and he bets $500. He rolls the dice and it lands on a 1, and he wins again, so now Chance has $1000! Chance feels invincible like he can not lose, so he decides to bet it all again on the third bet expecting the same perfect results. Chance bets the full amount he has of $1000, but this time he lands on a 6 and loses it all.

The odds were in Chance's favor all along, but he still lost everything because he bet more then he could afford to lose multiple times (he broke the 3rd golden rule of investing, he put all his eggs in one basket by betting it all on one risky bet).

An hour later Frank comes back and sees Chance again with the same long look on his face sitting at the now empty table in the middle of the casino, and Frank hears from one of his workers that Chance has lost all his money again. Frank goes over to Chance who tells him exactly what happened a couple hours earlier. Frank says, "I know you have to do things your way, but I would suggest not to bet everything on every bet." Then Frank smiled and said, "I have learned that life is about what we do with the chances we receive, and it is also about learning from each chance we get. And sometimes in life a wonderful and rare thing happens, sometimes life gives you a second chance!"

Frank then smiled and said, "I still want you to win, maybe you have learned something from your loss. Let me give you a second chance with the odds in your favor again." Frank then gives Chance just a hundred dollars to try again." This time Chance has learned from his loss, so he decides to bet $25 over and over instead of betting it all each time. And within a couple hours Chance has over $5000.00, he increases his bet to $250, and a couple hours later he wins a total of $50,000, and then he bets $2500 at a time. Soon he has accumulated $300,000, and then he decides to bet $10000 at a time, and a short time later he actually wins the full amount! Chance is overjoyed as he has won the full amount that corresponds to his 10/5 birthday, a 10 followed by 5 zeros, or $1,000,000!

Chance has learned this day that building wealth involves more then just having the odds in your favor, it also involves limiting *your losses, because no matter how good the odds are, and no matter how lucky you have been in the past, sometimes you lose.*

Why did Chance lose all his money during the first chance he was given, and then win a fortune with the second chance he was given? Nothing changed about the odds of winning, and on his second chance, he even started with less money. Chance started with only $100 on his second chance, compared to $250 at the start of his first chance. The difference is that Chance realized something that is the same in gambling as it is in investing, it is that even if the odds are in your favor, *sometimes you lose.* So just as golden rule # 3 above states, it is best to only invest what you can afford to lose multiple times before you win in any one risky investment.

The greatest obstacle to beginning investors is the temptation to invest everything into one high risk investment. In the short term a risky stock may go up, the next high risk stock bought may also go up, but it is likely that eventually a high risk stock will go down, or even crash, destroying the profits and the initial investment. The feeling of invincibility, similar to the expectation of investment perfection, often leads to financial disaster.

Financial disaster is the long term result of ignoring the 3rd golden rule of investing listed above by putting all your money in one risky investment. This is because **no matter how good the odds of winning may be each time you make an investment, sometimes you lose.**

For those who are scientifically or mathematically inclined there is a formula that one can use to estimate the average return on an investment. We can estimate the average return on an investment if we can figure out the probability of a win and a loss. For example in the above story Chance wins 4 out of six times and loses 2 out of six times. So we could use a formula to calculate the average total profit each bet would generate in the bets time frame. My formula that I use to estimate potential profits on investments I have named "The Average Profit Formula."

The Average Profit Formula is: A(P-L)=AP

Amount invested = A

Potential Profit = P

Potential Loss = L

Average Profit =AP

So the formula for calculating the average likely profit on an investment or a gambling bet is the dollar amount times the result of the chance to win minus the chance of a loss, or A(P-L)=AP.

So using the same odds as the story above, if Chance had the chance of winning 4 out of six times he rolls a six sided dice, and if we use the bet amount of $300, then with this formula we can estimate what his average profit for each bet would be:

$300 (4/6 - 2/6) which is simplified to $300(2/6), or $300(1/3), or $100. So if

Chance bet $300 with the odds in his favor then his average profit per roll is $100. Each roll may be a win or a loss, but over time the average profit would approximate $100 per roll. So if he rolls the dice10 times betting $300, then he would likely make an average profit of $1000. Random chance may make it more or less, but over time the average returns on each bet would eventually approximate the average profit formula.

Next let's discuss the secrets of creating long term profits with various investments and investment strategies.

So how do the three golden rules of investing work in the world of stocks? Here is an example, imagine if a man with $10000.00 decides to invest everything he has in one stock at a time. The first stock goes up 50%, then he buys another stock that goes up 25%, then he buys another stock that goes up 25%, and then the next stock he buys goes down 50%, and the next stock he buys goes down 50%. The question is how much money would he have? Looking at the percentages one would assume the man would break even, but that is not how it works in reality:

$10000 up 50% = $15000

$15000 up 25% = $18750

$18750 up 25% = $23437.50

$23437.50 down 50% = $11718.75

$11718.75 down 50% = $5859.38

So even though the investments went up a total of 100% and down a total of 100% (the same percentage up as it went down), the investor still lost over 40% of their beginning balance. Over time this type of investing method ("All Eggs in One Basket" - all of one's money in one risky stock) will usually destroy one's savings.

The reason behind the greater loss when someone puts all their money in one risky investment is simple. In the above example the man will usually have more money invested when the stock goes down then when the stock goes up. If they make a lot on a stock then they invest more in the next stock, so when they hit the stock that goes down the investment is greater which increases their loss. Then after each loss they have less money to invest the next time, so even if the next stock goes up the same percentage as the last stock went down, they profit less and have less money then they started with. And continuing this type of investing will normally cause one's balance to continually drift down.

The key to consistent long term gains is to have both a winning investment strategy, and to diversify investments so the amount invested when a stock goes up is at least equal to the amount invested when a stock goes down. One way to do this is to invest the same amount in multiple stocks over and over again, the idea is the amount invested when a loss occurs will be equal to the amount invested for a win. For example, let's look at the same example as above but keep the amount invested in each stock the same throughout the period of time:

$10000 up 50% = balance of $15000

$10000 up 25% = balance of $17500

$10000 up 25% = balance of $20000

$10000 down 50% = balance of $15000

$10000 down 50% = balance of $10000

In the same example if the investment in each stock was the same amount of $10000.00, then the ending balance would be the same $10000.00, instead of the smaller balance of $5859.38 that investing everything in each stock would create.

If one manages the amount invested to be the same after each win or loss, then the key to profits will be to invest in stocks that are more likely to go up, or more likely to go up a greater amount, then they are likely to go down. The secrets to finding these, and other highly profitable investments, will be discussed a little later.

Even if someone knows how to find stocks that are more likely to go up the majority of the time, the temptation to invest 100% in one volatile stock can lead to disaster, especially with leveraged margin investing. To illustrate this let's say if 80% of the time a new stock goes up 50%, but 20% of the time the new stock goes down 50%. And let's assume one uses margin buying power to borrow money so they can invest 2x what they have, or 200% of their equity. Here is a likely result of investing everything in each stock using margin buying power and with the odds greatly in one's favor:

Day 1: $10000 initial equity, but margin investing allows the investor to buy twice as much stock, or $20000. After the first stock goes up 50% the investor would have $30000 worth of stock minus $10000 borrowed (margin money), which means they would have a $20000 balance at the end of the 1st day. And repeating the process with all of the money would likely result similarly to what follows here:

Day 2: $20000 balance, so $40000 invested in 2nd stock using margin, stock goes up 50%, so the ending balance is $40000.

Day 3: $40000 balance now so $80000 of 3rd stock bought using margin goes up 50%, so ending balance $80000.

Day 4: $80000 balance now so $160000 of
4th stock bought using margin goes up 50%,
so ending balance $160000.

Day 5: $160,000 balance now so $320000 of
5th stock bought using margin, but this is the
one out of 5 times that the stock goes down.
A 50% loss on $320000 is $160000. So the
ending balance is $0.

$0 is the ending balance! So all the money
was lost even though 4 out of 5 times the
stocks went up 50%, and only once went
down 50%! Not understanding this simple
principle of margin investing destroys so
many people's life savings in the stock
market, and in other investments. With
margin buying power, even if the odds of
profit are greatly in one's favor, the
expectation of perfection leaves no
investment protection, and it eventually leads
to great financial imperfection.

Expecting perfection in investing is like
driving full speed up a hill toward the edge of
a cliff, one's money balance in the short term
goes up, but eventually it leads to disaster
when they reach the edge of the cliff and

encounter the stock that falls off the cliff. No one is going to be right with every investment, and this is why diversification of risk is an important key to investing, and it is also the key to maintaining long term continuous profits.

On the other hand if someone uses both diversification and has a winning stock investment strategy, then the results would likely be much different. Using the same example above with the same winning odds but using multiple stocks instead of one risky stock at a time, would likely give the following result:

In this next example the investor starts with the same initial savings of $10000, the same winning odds and margin buying power, but they also diversify investments. They invest in five stocks using 2x margin (total of $20,000), with $4000 going into each of the 5 different stocks. 4 of 5 stocks go up 50% and one goes down 50%, just like the previous example but with some diversification which limits the risk. Here is a likely result:

Day 1: $10000 starting balance, with margin of 2X investment or $20,000 that is invested in five stocks. 4 stocks go up 50% generating $8000 of profit - but one stock goes down 50% creating a loss of $2000. So the total overall profit is $6000. So after day one the total balance is $16000.

Repeating above with same return as the above example (4 of 5 stocks going up 50%, and one stock going down 50%) would get a consistent 60% gain and the following results:

Day 2: $16000 to $25600

Day 3: $25600 to $40960

Day 4: $40960 to $65536

Day 5: $65536 to $104857.60

Same odds and returns on stocks, over same time frame, and starting with same $10000 - leaves one investor with $0 as in earlier example, and this investor with $104857.60. The difference in the results is simply because the later investor diversified risk by not putting all their money in one risky stock.

A caution with margin investments and the stock market - even with diversification in stocks, on some days almost all stocks can drop drastically during the day or over night, this could also destroy one's savings. Therefore if one decides to use margin investing, it is less risky from open to close of the market where one can usually limit the total loss to a small percentage of the total investment. For example a person might use a stop market order during the day to invest using margin into a stock they feel is more likely to go up then down, so they create a profit potential while limiting risk of total loss to a small percentage of their savings because of being able to automatically sell during the day if the market suddenly drops or crashes.

An additional note with stock investing, one needs to be aware of how to buy close to the bid price and how to sell close to the ask price, such as using limit orders and high volume stocks, to avoid losing money whenever getting in and out of stocks if they trade frequently. One can have the right investing strategy, but if they lose too much money buying or selling each stock then they can still go broke.

Of course in the real world an investment gain of 2 out of 4 stocks of 10%, and a loss in 2 out of 4 stocks of 5% may be closer to the reality of an advanced stock trader following a stock trend, and the returns may be over days, weeks, or months instead of a day. But the same principle above applies, and can still make one wealthy, very quickly.

The key to successful long term investing in stocks is both seeking investments with high profit potential while simultaneously limiting the risk of loss by limiting the total amount invested in each stock. There are many different strategies one can use or even develop on their own by researching stock price patterns, but the key always remains to diversify risk in order to hold on to gains.

The same golden rules of investing that apply to successful stock investing also applies to other investments. We always want to have an understanding of our odds of profit verses our odds of loss on our investments. We should only invest when the odds for profit are in our favor, and only invest an amount that we can afford to lose multiple times in any one risky investment.

Diversification of investments is crucial to maintaining wealth because life and world events are unpredictable, and things change over time. What may be a good investment today can easily change to a bad investment tomorrow.

Now we have covered how to get a job, how to start and grow a business, how to manage our money, and even how to make more money for our time; but what about our relationships?

Next we will learn about something that is so important to our life, but that we are never educated on in school. We will now look into how to build strong positive relationships.

How to Build Strong Positive Relationships

Our relationships can bring us joy, or they can break our heart. I remember very little being taught about relationships in school and college, just like many other things in life, this is something I had to figure out on my own. Fortunately you can benefit from the powerful relationship secrets that I have learned in the decades since my graduation.

If we are able to have strong and positive relationships with others it makes our life more enjoyable. The key to strong positive relationships begins with understanding who we want a relationship with, and how to treat them.

Strong positive relationships come from respecting others, having regular communication, and doing things that bring joy to others. And the best relationships are based on love.

Think about what type of person you would like to be around. If someone was always complaining about you, negative about everything you do with them, and always expecting you to do everything for them - how long would that relationship last, and how would it make you feel?

Our time is limited, and so if we value it, we have to carefully choose the people who we spend our time with. We may not have a choice of who our relatives are, or about everyone we may work with, but we can choose our friends, and we can usually choose who we spend our leisure time with.

We need to make sure the friends we choose to spend our leisure time with are worth our time. We can ask questions about our relationships to identify if the people we are around support our happiness, or if they are a negative relationship: Are we usually uplifted by being around them? Do our friends usually relieve our stress, or do they regularly add to our stress? Are we able to be ourself around our friends, or do we feel like we must pretend to be someone else? Are we the one that always has to do things for our friends, or do they also do things for us? Does spending time with our friends make us happy? So to sum it up, if our friends usually make us tense, angry, insecure about ourself, or sad; then we need to find new friends.

To make room for strong positive relationships, we may need to eliminate negative relationships. We need to value our own happiness and peace of mind. So if any of our relatives only negatively impact our happiness and they are not a part of our household, then we may need to limit, or completely eliminate, the time we spend around them.

Many times we may be able to improve the relationship with those who have brought us down, but sometimes we can not and thus we need to avoid the negative experience. The point is that we that must value our time and our happiness, and when we value our happiness then we become aware that we have no obligation to spend our leisure time around anyone who brings us down, even if they are relatives.

Now that we know who to spend time with and who to avoid, let's look at some things we can do to have a strong and positive relationship with those we have chosen to spend time with.

The first secret to building positive relationships lies in being aware of how we make others feel.

There are three keys to building strong positive relationships - positive actions and honest communication, having balance in our relationships, and putting in the effort.

The first step towards strengthening our relationships is to look at how we make others feel. We can ask ourselves some questions to see how well we are treating others: "How do my words and actions affect the emotional well-being of the other person in the relationship? Would my comments make someone feel valued or worthless? If someone said to me what I just said to them would it bring me joy, or sadness? How would I feel if I was treated the way I just treated others? And what words and actions do I use to intentionally bring joy to others?"

We also need to do some self-reflection to better understand our relationships. If we continually have trouble with those we are in a relationship with, then the trouble is not with the others, it is with us! How we treat others will affect whether others want to continue in a relationship with us. Many relationships end because one or both parties just don't know how to communicate with others. There is something rarely if ever taught in schools or universities, but it is extremely important to making relationships last and creating love in relationships; it is critical that we understand how to honestly communicate in a positive way.

We need to first be honest with ourself about the type of relationship we want to have with someone else, whether it is a friendship or a romantic relationship, or whether it is a short term relationship or a lifelong relationship. We also need to be honest with the other person in the relationship so that both of the people in the relationship have realistic expectations, and to help prevent either person from getting hurt. If someone has no desire to get married, but the person they are in a romantic relationship with does, then withholding this information from the other person will likely result in them being harmed. If someone is only interested in a one night stand, but pretends they want a long term relationship then they are driving towards the edge of a relationship cliff, and someone will inevitably get hurt when their expectations crash down.

Not only do we need honesty at the beginning of a relationship, we need to have day to day honesty during a relationship. This is the tricky part about honesty that is rarely taught in any school or university - some types of honesty hurt relationships and other types of honesty strengthen relationships. So we need to understand the type of honesty needed to maintain and strengthen relationships. Specifically, **we need to understand how to use what I refer to as positive honesty, and how to avoid using negative honesty.**

Negative honesty described here is telling someone everything you do not like about them, everything they did wrong, every physical flaw in their body, and every way they fall short of your personal expectation of perfection. Negative honesty does not really help anyone, it is just negative criticism.

Positive honesty is telling people why they are special to you, it is telling them and others all the wonderful things they do, talking about their desirable qualities, and giving helpful feedback on something they can improve. Positive honesty does not skip telling someone when they do something wrong or that is offensive to us, but it involves doing it in a way that is more likely to help someone improve or change, then it is likely to offend them. An example of each type of honesty is as follows:

Negative honesty: You eat too much and you are fat!

Positive honesty: You are drinking too much high sugar and high calorie soda, and you are eating too many bags of high fat and high calorie potato chips everyday, and this is affecting your weight and your health.

In the above example calling someone fat may be your honest personal opinion of them, but it does not typically make someone feel good about themselves, or motivate them to change. Additionally the person already knows how they look, and may become even more self conscious about it. The name calling aspect is also negative because saying someone IS fat is like labeling the entire value of one's physical appearance as bad, even though they may indeed be very physically attractive, but just not at what you feel to be the perfect weight. Additionally, name calling is like stamping the entire person with the label of FAT, which may easily be interpreted by that person as a judgement of their entire self worth as being bad. So this type of negative honesty only serves to kick a person over and over, and then to continually stomp on them when they are down; it does not help anyone, it simply weakens the relationship.

The example above of *positive honesty* avoids negative name calling, but instead focuses on the actions of the person that are destructive and need to be changed. This type of communication is more likely to motivate positive change, and less likely to offend or discourage the other person in the relationship. This is because you are not labeling the person or their looks as bad, but you are focusing on the actions that need to change, and it is easier for someone to consider changing an action then it is to consider changing the essence of who they are.

Here is another example of the two types of honesty that parents may use when talking to their young children:

Negative honesty: You are stupid! You got an "F" in math on your report card! You will never amount to anything with grades like that!

Positive honesty: You did not study or do your math homework in the last few months which caused you to get a failing grade in math on your report card. Let's plan on spending 15-30 minutes each day, either with me or with a tutor, going over your math assignments. With a little effort you can greatly improve your grade, and knowing math will help you to succeed at whatever you decide to do in life.

How do the above examples of the parents response to a failing math grade play out? Negative honesty in the above example labels the child as "stupid." It is an attack on who the child is, and may easily be seen as an attack on their value as a person. It gives no way forward, no hope for change, and it weakens the parent child relationship. But positive honesty focuses on the actions that caused the failing grade without labeling the child as stupid. It points to a way forward, to how simple it would be to change one's actions and the grade, and it points out that making a change will lead to a better future for the child. It gives hope for the future to the child, it encourages the child, and it strengthens the parent child relationship.

And a third example of the difference between the types of honest is seen by looking at the focus of our statements about others:

Negative Honesty: You are too short. You are too tall. Your skin is too dark. Your skin is too light.

Positive Honesty: (saying nothing)

Or an alternative Positive Honesty: You are too funny. You are too smart. You are too beautiful. You are too much fun to be around.

If our communication with others focuses on any possible flaw or perceived imperfection in others then we will make statements, which may be our honest opinion of someone, but that serve no purpose except to put down someone or to make them feel insecure.

For example, looking at the above example of saying, "You are too short." This is putting a negative label on someone and serves no constructive purpose. The person has no control over their height, so this statement can not encourage positive change. The person you called short, already knows their height, and they may easily feel you are attacking their value as a person. The person may become even more insecure and uncomfortable about their appearance. And the relationship with that person can easily become damaged.

Additionally, when we express our personal biased opinion about what physical qualities we feel someone should have by saying someone is too tall, short, dark, or light; it serves no useful purpose, it is just our opinion based on our expectation of what perfection is. Many others may disagree with our opinion of others. The same qualities one person hates, another person may love, so who can really say what is better? And it is a pointless negative attack because the person can not change how tall or short they are, or change the color of their skin; it is who they are. So this type of honesty is negative honesty, and the only purpose it serves is to hurt others and to destroy relationships.

On the other hand we can choose the positive honesty of saying nothing. We do not need to point out and focus on everything about others that we feel is imperfect. When we reframe from negative honesty, or criticism, then we are protecting our relationship and the feelings of the other person.

The other alternative positive honesty example is when we say something that we like about someone else. Again, the person who is short in our opinion does not need us to tell them this, they already know their height, and so do we. The same person who is short according to our opinion of perfection, will likely have other desirable qualities that we can point out, things like in the example above. The same person who we feel is short may be beautiful, funny, smart, and fun to be around. Why can't we point out one or more of their desirable qualities instead of attacking one aspect of their appearance that is meaningless to their value as a person, and that they have no control over?

Positive honesty is choosing to focus mostly on what we perceive to be the good in others, and it is more. Positive honesty also allows us to give constructive criticism of the actions of others that we disapprove of, but it avoids labeling the entire person as "bad", or labeling a person based on a physical or mental characteristic that they have no control over. Positive honesty gives a way forward. Positive honesty even allows us to say nothing, when we have nothing good or constructive to say. Positive honesty strengthens relationships and creates more love in our relationships.

Now that we know what to say to build strong positive relationships. But there are a couple more things we can do for our relationships, we can also seek balance in our relationships and put in the effort.

In addition to positive honesty, we need to have balance in our relationships. In other words, every relationship has a give and take aspect to it, so in order to function well and to last there needs to be some sort of equality in the contributions and actions from both parties. We can ask some questions to see how balanced we are in our relationships. Is our communication balanced, do we allow others to talk and do we listen to what they have to say; or are we more consumed with doing all the talking and making our point? Do we value the opinion of others, or do we insist on making others agree with all of our opinions? Do we always decide what activities we will do with our friends, or do we often let them decide? Do we always expect the other person to pay for things, or do we sometimes pay? Do we always expect the other person to initiate interactions, or to come up with the ideas of what to do together?

Balance in a relationship does not mean each person must do equal amounts of everything, it just means that each person must strive to contribute to what they do together.

And finally let's look at the effort and time we put into our relationships. Our relationships may start off great, but as the years go by we may gradually start to ignore the other person in subtle ways. We may even stop making an effort to get together with the other person. It may not be intentional, it is just that we may not realize how the flow of time and lack of interaction allows our close affections and warm memories to gradually drift away. But if we take the time and regularly put in the effort then we can create more love in our relationships, and this will contribute to our ongoing happiness.

Our relationships will strengthen when we take the time and make the effort to do nice things for others. We need to look at what we do to understand who we are affecting our relationships with others: do we occasionally compliment something we like about them, do we regularly keep in touch and communicate, do we remember important dates in their life, do we occasionally give them a gift or treat them to a meal, do we try to be available when they are in need, do we make an effort to make them enjoy the time spent together?

It is amazing how even a little effort, like doing something nice and unexpected, can brighten someone's day, strengthen our relationship, and can make us happy too.

Next we will look into something vital to our life that we are rarely educated on in school, our fitness and health.

How to Stay Fit & Healthy

In your life before and after graduation you are bombarded by advertising for every kind of diet gimmick to lose weight, there is even greedy attempts to get you to use all kinds of toxic drugs and vanity treatments which are supposed to make you fit and healthy. But these things generally have nothing to do with your health and fitness, and the side affects of the drugs actually destroy your health! Yet most educational institutions never teach us about these dangers, or how we can live a healthy fit life. As a result too many people fall victim to popping toxic pills, injecting toxins into their body, and seeking unnatural surgeries.

But the truth that I learned after graduation is that the secret to fitness and health is not a secret at all, it is directly related to some very specific things that we can control which we will cover next. We control our fitness and health by: **what we eat and drink, the exercise we get, and the sleep we get.**

What We Eat and Drink

Food makes up the building blocks of our body and supplies our energy. Living a life with unhealthy food and drinks is like driving a boat with holes in the bottom of it. A boat with holes leaking water may seem normal at first, but as time goes on it gets heavier, the engine floods, it eventually stops altogether, and it finally sinks. If we put destructive foods into our body then just like the boat we will slow down, break down, and stop altogether. But we can sail through our life with good health when we seal up the holes in our diet. We will improve our physical health by improving our eating and drinking habits, and when we have a plan based on the right knowledge, it actually becomes easy to do.

How does one eat healthy food at home? The battle to eat healthy at home is actually won or lost outside of the home, the battle is won by the foods we bring into our home to begin with. If our home is filled with unhealthy foods, then we are setting ourself up for failure. Most people know the difference between healthy and unhealthy foods, the problem is they buy the wrong types of foods in the first place. Once the unhealthy foods are embedded in one's home, then the battle to eat healthy becomes a difficult uphill battle.

The key to eating healthy is to shop for healthy foods only, even our snacks and desserts can be healthy (made with natural ingredients and having little or no additives and preservatives) while still delicious. When we shop for healthy foods that we also enjoy, then we are making it easy for us to succeed. We must start with buying the right foods for our home. This means we have to take a little bit of time and effort to think of the foods that we like which are also healthy for us. We need to understand if our food has unhealthy additives, chemicals, or excess sugar; this means we should actually look at the labels showing the ingredients. When we have the right healthy foods that we also enjoy in our home, then we are creating the right environment to succeed at eating healthy.

Freshness is a big part of eating healthy too. We need to check the expiration dates, and be mindful of the freshness of the food we consume. Some people buy fresh food, but then let the food sit out in the open air for hours before consuming it, making a once healthy good tasting food, spoiled and unhealthy. We need to check the dates when food is purchased and make sure to properly store food to keep it fresh until it is eaten. Some people may put foods that quickly spoils in an air tight container, or in the refrigerator, or in their freezer until they are ready to eat. So if we eat at home or on the go, we need to be aware of the freshness of the food we eat because fresh food is healthier for us, and it will taste better too.

If we eat on the go frequently, then we need to look at how to eat healthy food on the go. Restaurants usually have a variety of options, some of which are better for our health then others. We need to limit, or reduce, the items we know are destructive to our health, and we need to choose the healthier options. Instead of buying expensive soda at drive through restaurants, one could drink water by keeping bottled water, or a water bottle, in their car with them to drink with the food they eat on the go. Instead of getting the largest burger with extra cheese and mayonnaise, one could control portion size by ordering a regular sized burger and removing items high in fat like mayonnaise or extra cheese, especially if they do not crave them. Another way to eat healthy on the go is to add healthier foods to our diet, we can eat a salad or vegetables with each meal which will leave us less room to eat unhealthy food on the go.

Successful healthy eating is not based on depriving ourself of every food we enjoy, it is about eating a variety of foods including foods that we may crave like desserts, but in the right proportion. A healthy diet does not exclude desserts, it just limits the amount of dessert relative to the total amount of food we eat. We should eat a variety of foods so that our bodies get a broad variety of nutrients, and we should seek to have the right proportion of the different types of food. So instead of eating mostly sweets in our diet, we need to eat a small proportion of sweets. Or instead of just eating fruits all day, we need to eat a balance of fruits, vegetables, dairy, breads and cereals and meats. Having balanced eating habits does not mean we can not eat high sugar or high fat foods, it just means that we need to make these foods a smaller proportion of our total diet. So if we replace a high sugar soda with a water, we may be able to eat a dessert, and still be in balance. If we avoid a high salt main dish we may be able to have some french fries with some salt on them, while still being in balance. When we are not deprived of the foods we love the most, then we make it easier to maintain our healthy eating habits indefinitely.

Another key to eating healthy lies in how much we eat during each meal, or our portion size. Whether we eat at home or on the go, we need to be aware of our portion size. If we eat huge portions of food we are forcing our body to get bigger by storing excessive fat, and we are putting a great stress on our heart and digestive system. But by simply eating smaller portions more frequently throughout the day, our body does not have to store excessive fat, our digestion and circulation is better, we don't feel sluggish, and we will have more energy.

Small portions that are large enough to make us feel full, but that do not make us feel stuffed is best. It takes about 2-3 hours to digest what we eat, so many health experts recommend to eat more frequently, for example 6 times a day with three meals and a small snack between each meal. Many people make the mistake of starving all day and then eating one large meal a day, but this forces the body to store fat because of going into survival mode until the next meal. But when we eat small portions more frequently then this keeps our bodies lean because our metabolism keeps burning calories faster throughout the whole day.

What foods are good for our health? It is no secret that our body needs nutrients that are normally supplied in the four basic food groups - meats, dairy, breads and cereals, and fruits and vegetables. Everyone will not have the same diet as each of us crave different foods, but fortunately there are many ways to eat healthy. We can also eat healthy with a vegetarian or non-dairy diet as long as we include other foods that provide the nutrients we are not getting from meat or dairy foods.

Some diets seem healthy, but can be harmful to our health. Many people feel eating a salad is healthy, but if they just eat lettuce and celery and smother it with salad dressing which is made mostly of fat, then they may actually be harming their health and gaining excess weight. Since the salad is lacking multiple vegetables and full of high fat salad dressing it may actually make someone gain more weight then if they ate a burger and fries, all the while still leaving them feeling hungry, and leaving their body malnourished. A healthy salad would have more then just lettuce and dressing - it would be made with fresh ingredients, it would be full of multiple different colorful vegetables, it may include a topping of some protein foods like meat or chopped up boiled eggs, and topped with light salad dressing to add flavor. It would not only taste great, but it would also be great for your health.

The foundation of our health is built on what we eat and drink, if we make the effort to get the details right with what we consume, then we can have the health we seek and we can also enjoy delicious foods.

To get the full health benefits of our foods we also need to eat foods that are free from unhealthy preservatives, additives, or chemicals. We must be aware of how our food is made because some food producers care little about the consumer's health and they cut corners to make a greater profit. Some food producers may put unhealthy preservatives, additives, or even chemicals in the food they make. We must take a moment to read labels and research unknown ingredients to protect our health, and the health of our family.

A variety of foods provide a variety of nutrients which is very good for our health. We need to avoid eating too much of one type of food, or the same exact meal over and over. We all have our favorite foods to eat, but the key to healthy eating lies in the balance of eating a variety of foods. So although we can eat our favorites more often, we need to make sure to add different types of foods to our diet. Variety creates a larger pool of nutrients that our bodies can use to stay healthy. If a person loves pizza but they have pizza for every meal then it becomes unhealthy, because their diet lacks variety. But if a person has a variety of different foods in a week and they include the pizza they love on a couple of the days, then they can enjoy their favorite food frequently and still get a healthy variety of foods in their total diet for the week.

The key to eating desserts and snacks is balance. We need balance to control the amount of unhealthy snacks and desserts we eat. If we fill up on a healthy meal, we can still have some desserts and snacks as long as we eat a balanced portion. The key to success is to fill up on healthy foods first so we have less room and desire for unhealthy foods, or for excessive desserts that may contain high sugar and high fat. We can also seek a higher quality of snacks as we balance our diet by choosing snacks that have little or no preservatives or unnatural additives.

The belief that healthy food tastes bad is another barrier many people have when trying to eat healthy. Many people believe that healthy food does not taste good because of misinformation and false beliefs. This barrier is an imaginary one based on misconceptions of what healthy foods are. Healthy foods actually are every type of food such as breads and cereals, fruits and vegetables, meats and dairy products. It is just that healthy food is made from natural ingredients, free of additives and chemicals, it contains a small or balanced amount of fat and sugar, and it is fresh when consumed. Unhealthy food can not compare to the wonderful taste of healthy food! And when someone understands that GREAT tasting food is also healthy food this barrier to healthy eating no longer exits!

Many people do not want to try to eat healthy because they believe the opposite is true, they think a healthy diet is just eating celery all day. We must change our perspectives on what is healthy food to succeed at healthy eating. Healthy food and eating healthy does not involve only eating unappealing vegetables, it actually involves eating a huge variety of great tasting foods and desserts. If our food is fresh, does not contain harmful chemicals or preservatives, does not contain an unbalanced amount of sugar or fat, and has a variety of nutrient rich ingredients; then we will both enjoy our food more and we will stay healthy.

One additional and important note needs to be mentioned regarding what we consume. Even if we are eating healthy we can still destroy our health if we pollute our body with drugs. We also need to avoid unnecessary drugs to stay healthy. A drug is normally not a nutrient, and it is normally harmful to the normal healthy functioning of the human body over time. Much of the world has large drug companies that sell drugs for profit. It is much more profitable to make drugs to treat a condition over and over again for a patient's life, then it is to sell a one time cure. Their is also the temptation for doctors in countries like the US to prescribe a drug for every condition, instead of telling patients they need to change their habits to eat healthy foods, to get enough sleep, and to get enough exercise. Doctors may prescribe a drug because they assume the patient will not change their eating, exercise, and sleep habits. Also they may feel they are protected from a lawsuit by following the routine drug prescription policy that most doctors do. The problem is that most drugs are unnatural and have side effects which require other drugs, all of which usually does cumulative harm to the body. So we should ask our doctor about alternatives to drugs, like changes to our lifestyle, instead of always defaulting to taking yet another drug. And we need to be willing to change our habits so that we do not become dependent on drugs.

Sometimes drugs are needed for some conditions, usually for a limited period of time. But many drugs can be addictive and can be extremely dangerous, especially over time. So we need to ask ourselves, and our doctors, if all of the drugs that we are taking are absolutely necessary. And we need to check if there is some natural change to our lifestyle and eating habits that we can take, instead of taking an unnatural drug.

In many countries people live longer without having the drugs treatments from high technology medical centers as in richer countries like the US. The only big difference appears to be the natural foods they eat, and their active lifestyle. **The point is that the real key to our health seems to come from the foods we regularly eat, the exercise we get, the sleep we get, and our environment; good health is unlikely to ever be contained in the many unnatural drugs promoted by drug companies who are trying to make a profit.**

Natural healthy foods and exercise can cure many ailments. Many people have found that changing what they eat has made them healthy from ailments that many other people take drugs for most of their life. Diabetes has been cured for some by reducing sugar in their diet, eliminating soda, and getting regular exercise. Some people with asthma who adopt a rigorous exercise routine have been cured of asthma. Others who suffer from obesity have simply changed their diet and added exercise habits to create a complete transformation in their body and health. Natural healthy foods and exercise may not automatically cure everyone of every ailment, but it is the right first step to take on the path to our health.

What we drink is very important to our health too. Many people drink excessive amounts of alcohol or soda. Alcohol in large amounts is very destructive to our health. Soda may seem innocent, but it is extremely dangerous in large amounts because of the excessive sugar and/or chemicals it contains. But something as simple as drinking a cup of water with each meal, can change a person's life. If we eliminate or cut down on the soda and alcoholic drinks we consume, our physical health will benefit. We can increase our health if we replace soda or alcohol with clean water at each meal. We also can substitute natural drinks, like natural juices with our meals, instead of drinking an excessive amount of alcohol. Many people who have suffered from diabetes and excessive weight, have eliminated diabetes and obesity by simply eliminating excessive soda drinking, and adding aerobic exercise to their daily routine. And even if the right eating and exercise habits do not cure many from a disease like diabetes, it can still greatly improve one's health.

Other things to avoid in order to protect our health are sugar substitutes. We should avoid sugar substitutes in our drinks and food because it is a dangerous gamble. In the past many sugar substitutes have later been shown to cause cancer or have other dangerous side effects, and some may even increase weight gain more then sugar. Only time will tell for many artificial unnatural substitutes released to the public. But why risk our health on something that is not fully proven to be safe, or on something that may later be determined to be deadly?

The influence of our eating habits on our health can be dramatic over our entire life. Everything we regularly do matters, and each seemingly insignificant bad habit can wreck our health over time. Imagine if two twins grew up with different eating habits. Next is an illustration about what might happen to two identical twins who choose different eating habits.

Fast Meal and Thoughtful Meal

A first born twin, called Fast Meal, eats unhealthy fast food with lots of fat and salt, and drinks high sugar soda with each meal. While the second born twin, Thoughtful Meal, eats healthy meals with some vegetables and fruit, and drinks water with each meal. And they both eat similar desserts. Here is how their lives unfold:

The first twin, Fast Meal, has typical eating habits of many people. He has a soda with each meal, orders a super sized portion at fast food restaurants, he eats high fat and salty fast food frequently, and tops each meal off with a large amount of high sugar dessert. Fast Meal chooses to put no time, thought, or effort into selecting healthy foods; instead he just does what is the quickest, easiest, and most convenient item available whenever he selects his food. Each year Fast Meal gains weight, and over the years he has to continually buy bigger clothes to fit his ever expanding body.

Fast Meal makes his diet decisions based on what seems cheap, fast, and easy. He eats inexpensive fast food almost all the time as he does not want make the effort, or take the time, to prepare any of his own food. And his snacks at home also are cheap and easy. For example, Fast Meal regularly eats from a big bag of a popular brand of potato chips as he lays on the couch, and washes it down with high sugar soda. The popular brand of potato chips he eats actually bought up all the other companies with healthier brands of potato chips that his store used to offer, so they would be the only option. The few large soda companies also bought up many healthier drink options, so customers have to choose their unhealthy drinks. So when Fast Meal shops for chips he can only buy the same popular brand of unhealthy chips and unhealthy soda because it would be too difficult and time consuming to go to another store.

So partly because of his limited options and mostly because he does not want to put any time or effort into what he eats, Fast Meal continually lays on his couch and snacks on the chips that are high in fat and full of unhealthy preservatives and additives. And the soda he drinks is no joke, it is full of sugar and unhealthy additives with no nutritional value. So over time, this cheap, fast, and easy diet causes him to gain weight and to suffer from diabetes. The diabetes his eating habits cause then require a lifetime of continual, expensive, side effect filled treatments that cause continual pain.

As Fast Meal gains weight each year he has more trouble exercising, so he becomes more overweight. Eventually he becomes obese. Now he has to take medications because he refuses to change his eating and exercise habits, so his doctor feels that there is no choice but to prescribe more medications. The medications have side effects which then require more medications to treat. Fast Meal feels tired all the time, suffers from frequent head aches, and he even has trouble sleeping. He can not do all that he wants to do with the special people in his life because he is often tired, and regularly feels sick and unhealthy.

Fast meal is desperate for an easy and fast change to his weight, and so he easily falls victim to throwing his money away on various diet scams and ineffective exercise devices. He follows the eating advice of over weight out of shape TV hosts, he tries costly bad tasting pre-made diet meals, he tries various diet pills, and buys multiple random unusual exercise devices that he rarely uses; but none of these expensive gimmicks work. The problem is that Fast Meal never permanently changes his diet and does not regularly exercise, instead he lays on his couch eating his high fat bag of potatoes chips and makes no joke of drinking high sugar soda, all the while wondering why he can not lose weight. Fast Meal continues to gain weight and to suffer from health issues year after year.

As the years go by he has to have surgeries related to being overweight, and eventually he becomes disabled. He eventually requires a wheel chair because of trouble with his legs and feet. Fast Meal lives in pain for many years. His family and children try to care for him, and because of worrying about his health, they all suffer much stress and anxiety. And finally Fast Meal's life is cut short when his heart gives out because of the stress created by his extra weight and poor circulation. And because his eating habits are followed by some of his children, their health suffers too in the generations that follow.

Thoughtful Meal, in contrast to the first twin, chooses to put a little bit of thought and some time into selecting what he eats each day. Thoughtful Meal knows that changing one thing that he eats each day can make a big change in his overall fitness and health. He used to eat like Fast Meal as a child, but as an adult he started to make some changes to his diet. Thoughtful meal chooses to eat some vegetables and a variety of fruit each day, and this leaves less room and less cravings for unhealthy foods and desserts. Then he replaces high sugar soda with clean water, which also allows him to better taste and enjoy his meals. And he also changes his snacks to things like chips and cookies that are all natural with no chemicals, additives, preservatives, or excessive sugar. He finds that natural snacks can have less sugar and fat while still tasting better then what he would eat with Fast Meal as a kid.

Thoughtful Meal still eats some fast food but he selects healthy items to go with the meal, and he regularly prepares many healthy meals and snacks for himself. Because of his thoughtfulness in selecting and preparing his foods, Thoughtful Meal consumes better tasting fresh food without chemicals or unhealthy additives. The one change of drinking water with each meal instead of drinking soda prevents him from having high sugar level in his blood, so he never get diabetes. He also still gets to enjoy most of the foods he likes and a moderate amount of dessert each day. Thoughtful Meal eats some snacks, but unlike Fast Meal, he searches for healthy snacks.

Thoughtful Meal occasionally lays on the couch with a bag of potato chips, but he gets the chips that taste better then Fast Meal's chips. This is because he checks to make sure there is not a bunch of preservatives and additives and no excessive fat, so his potato chips actually taste better. He knows the danger of the popular soda Fast Meal drinks is no joke, so he does not fall prey to it. Thoughtful meal actually enjoys both better tasting and healthier foods then his twin. And since he does not become severely overweight, it is easier for him to exercise. Thoughtful Meal also has the energy each day to do the things he wants with the people he desires, like his children.

The healthy food and drink, along with Thoughtful Meal's regular exercise allows him to feel good, and it makes him physically able to really enjoy his life. He has more energy to work and to play his entire life. The second twin lives a longer, healthier, more productive and more joyful life; and his example is followed by many of his children and other family members, who also enjoy the same health benefits in their life. His fine example of how to enjoy the best tasting healthy food is followed by his children, his children's children, and other relatives; and it continues to help his family generation after generation, and all because he took a moment to put a little thought into what he was eating.

Just like the twins, we have a choice to be like Fast Meal, or to be like Thoughtful Meal. We can choose to put no thought, effort, or time into what we consume; or we can take control of our diet and our future. What we eat sets the stage for the type of life we will have and even how long we will live, so we need to choose healthy food and drinks so we can enjoy a long healthy life. With just a moment of thought and tiny bit of effort in choosing our food and drink, we can transform our body's fitness and increase our health.

The last thing to mention about what we choose to put into our bodies is that we should avoid ever using illegal drugs, and the excessive use of legal drugs like alcohol and tobacco. People in search of a high, or attempting to fit in with others, may drink excessive alcohol, smoke, or take illegal drugs. But if we value our health, then we will use moderation in drinking alcohol, we will avoid smoking anything, and we will never take illegal drugs.

Why is it important not to consume excessive amounts of alcohol? It is no secret that excessive alcohol consumption is dangerous to one's health, but many people forget that excessive alcohol may lead to bad decisions that harm ourself and others. How many people die because of drunk drivers? How many drunk people hurt others? The long term affect of alcohol abuse should also be considered. How many people ruin their liver and die early because of excessive alcohol consumption? Is it really worth getting a temporary artificial high to lose our rational decision making, to potentially ruin our health, to shorten our life, and to get sick and throw up the next day?

Some people take drugs or drink excessive amounts of alcohol to forget or hide from something else about themselves or their life. Are we really drinking excessively to hide from facing something else? We should seek support groups or counseling if we are struggling with alcohol for some unaddressed reason.

If we have good supportive friends, then they will understand, and they will never try to persuade us to consume excessive alcohol. We need to have people around us who support us and our health, we just should not hang out with people who try to persuade us to drink excessively. It will be easier to make the right decisions about drinking if we are around the right people, so we must also be aware of the company we keep.

In addition to alcohol we need to avoid smoking. Many people are lucky enough not to have the habit of smoking electronic cigarettes, cigarettes, or cigars. But for those addicted to smoking, they should seek to quit, or at least to limit how much they smoke. The substances in a cigar, cigarette, pipe, or electronic smoking device may be very harmful and can quickly ruin one's health, and long term they may lead to an early and miserable death. There are so many other healthy options to enjoy life besides smoking, why would someone choose to trap themselves in service to a filthy habit that consumes their money, attacks the health of everyone around them, and continually sucks away their life?

We also need to avoid illegal drugs for multiple reasons. Starting with the obvious, they are illegal and the penalty for using, or possessing, illegal drugs can be severe. Some people have received long prison sentences and have ruined their life for simply possessing a drug that was legal in one country or province, but illegal in another. Other people have taken an illegal drug one time as a naive kid, or as an adult, and died!

Illegal drugs have no regulations on how they are made, on the type of chemicals put in them, or on how much of a specific drug they contain. Thus what many may think is a harmless pill to get a high, may actually contain many more times the amount of a dangerous drug than anyone realizes. The harsh truth is that a seemingly harmless pill may kill anyone who takes it, even if it is their very first time taking an illegal drug. So if we are wise we will never use illegal drugs because we know that just trying an illegal drug ONE time can ruin our health, or even be deadly!

Our health will benefit when we put good things into our body. We need to eat a variety of healthy foods, multiple times a day, and in moderate portions to enjoy good health. We need to eat the right balance of foods, which means that we can still enjoy a moderate portion of desserts with a healthy meal. We need to avoid consuming excessive amounts of alcohol, high sugar foods, and high fat foods. And we also need to safeguard our health by not abusing legal drugs like alcohol or tobacco, and never using illegal drugs.

Consuming healthy food and drink and avoiding harmful drugs is the first step towards physical health, the next step involves the exercise we get.

The Exercise We Get

I never understood how important exercise was to my health and to my enjoyment of life when I graduated from college, this is something that all my childhood classes also seemed to skip. Next we will see why it is so important to exercise, and how we can easily incorporate it into our lives.

Our bodies need exercise to be healthy. If we roll out of bed, sit on the couch all day, and then roll back into bed with no exercise; then our future health is doomed. Lack of exercise can be even more deadly then smoking or excessive alcohol drinking.

Many people don't exercise because they feel it is too hard, others try to exercise one day a week and wonder why they don't see results. Our body is full of muscles and joints that need the regular stimulation of exercise to stay healthy. Exercise stimulates our cells health by increasing blood flow and oxygen to them. But if we do not exercise then our body breaks down and eventually even simple things like walking short distances will become difficult as our muscles, bones, joints, nerves, and heart deteriorate from lack of use. Our body may even get tired when we are inactive once we become weakened from lack of exercise. But when we exercise regularly our energy level throughout the day will be higher, we will not feel so tired, we will be able to do more things. And it is this ability to physically do the things we want in life that will give us a better enjoyment of our life.

The key to making exercise easy and effective is to incorporate exercise into our daily routine by adding the activities we enjoy. If we enjoy riding a bike, and add that to our daily routine, it makes it easy to exercise regularly which also will make our efforts to continually exercise more effective. If we enjoy going for a walk, and we add walking to our daily routine, then it makes it easy and effective to exercise just by walking each day. If we can not conveniently go to a gym, then we can incorporate exercising at home or at work. The easier and more routine we make it to exercise, the easier we make it for us to succeed at staying healthy. Even when we incorporate just one activity into our daily routine we make it easy to regularly exercise, to stay fit, and to stay healthy. And by doing activities we enjoy, we make it easier to stay motivated so that we can keep exercising day after day, and year after year. And the ultimate result of our consistency is that we get to enjoy a lifetime of greater fitness and health.

We will be more effective at exercising if we plan how we will exercise. We can create a weekly schedule of the activities we will participate in to get our exercise. When one actually plans their weekly schedule of activities it ensures regular exercise. For example, if someone enjoys walking outdoors, riding a bike, playing tennis, and lifting weights then they might create a schedule to incorporate the activities they enjoy into specific week days. On Sundays they might plan to go for a bike ride. On Monday, Wednesday, and Friday they might decide to do weight lifting. On Tuesday and Thursday they might plan to go for a walk outdoors. And on Saturday they might plan to play Tennis.

Any combination of activities will work for us, as long as we do regular and consistent exercise. We can plan our daily activities to make sure we get exercise. We can make a list of activities we enjoy and then incorporate them into our weekly routine to make it even easier and more consistent to get our exercise. Just planning to be active a short time, even 15 minutes each day, will make us healthier, and the overall affect can be life changing.

We have many options available to us to exercise throughout our day, even if we are busy. If someone realizes they watch several hours of TV each day, and they hate the commercials between shows, they may exercise on the commercials and in between shows a couple of minutes each time to easily get plenty of daily exercise.

Instead of one exercise for a long period of time, we can incorporate multiple exercises throughout our day. For some it may be more convenient to do exercise for very short periods of time, but multiple times in the day. Let's say someone working in an office all day wants to exercise during a busy day. They might walk for 5 minutes in the morning before going to work, play table tennis or catch with a frisbee with a co-worker for 15 minutes at lunch. And then walk 5 minutes during their last break. And during the weekend they may have more time and so they may play a sport like basketball or racket ball for 30 minutes on Saturday and Sunday. This way one is getting regular exercise each day doing what they enjoy and all conveniently within short periods of time during each work day, and longer periods of time during the weekends. If we think of exercise like we think of eating or brushing our teeth each day, then exercise will become just as routine and easy to do on a regular and consistent basis.

A final note on exercise is that we need to listen to our bodies when we decide which exercises to do, and how much exercise to do each day. Someone who never jogs should not expect that they can suddenly run a marathon. Many people ignore pain and try to do too much exercise at once, this often leads to injuries which may be serious, and which may prevent future exercise. Our bodies may be fighting an illness, or we may not have gotten enough sleep the prior night, or we may have strained a muscle earlier, etc.; the point is to make our exercise most effective we must listen to how our body feels each day so that we exercise enough, but not too much. We want to challenge but not injure our muscles when we exercise, which means we may need to reduce or eliminate certain exercises according to how our body feels each day.

Now that we know how to eat healthy and how to get regular exercise, we need to look at the last step towards physical health. We need to focus on the sleep we get.

The Sleep We Get

How many classes taught me about getting enough sleep? You guessed it zero! But sleep is so vital to the enjoyment of life and to our accomplishments that I sought to learn more about it after I graduated. Next we will discuss the secrets to getting enough sleep.

Sleep is necessary for our health. Living without sleep is like driving a gasoline car with no engine oil, the car runs normal for a little while then the engine overheats, the engine burns up, and then the car stops for good. Without enough sleep we are burning up our body, limiting our ability to accomplish the important things we want to accomplish in our life, and causing life shortening internal damage that may stop us for good! If we want to be active, to accomplish things in life, and to be healthy; then we need to oil our body engine by getting enough sleep.

The start of getting enough sleep is to go to sleep early enough to get enough sleep. If we have to get up at 7 AM, but choose to go to sleep at 2 AM, then we guarantee the failure of getting enough sleep. If the typical human sleep renewal cycle takes 8 hours, and it takes us 30 minutes on average to fall asleep, then we should be going to sleep by at least by 10:30 PM to get up at 7 AM. If we like to read in bed for an hour before we go to sleep, or to do some other activity before we go to sleep, then we need to also add the additional time into our calculation of when we go to bed, so that we have enough time to get enough sleep. Getting enough sleep starts first with allowing enough time to sleep.

Next we need to control our physical environment to support sleep. Ideally we need a comfortable, cool, quiet, dark environment to help us sleep. We can increase our sleeping comfort by adjusting one or more things such as the bed we sleep on, the bed covering, the sheets and the pillows. We may be able to adjust the thermostat to create a cool temperature when we sleep. We may create a quiet environment by changing where we live, who we live with, or by adding sound reduction materials to the place where we sleep. We can change window coverings, or in some cases the time we sleep, to create the dark environment we want to inspire sleep. Something as simple as a blindfold and ear muffs may also help many to create the quiet dark environment that is desired for sleep.

Additionally we may be able to schedule or set aside some personal time during the day when we can take a nap, for the times when we do not get enough sleep at night. While it is preferable to sleep 8 or more hours straight through, many times our daily obligations and circumstances may not allow it. So having occasional back up sleep plans can also help us stay healthy and productive.

Finally we need to know how to go to sleep. While we may not be able to force ourselves to immediately fall asleep, there are things we can do to make it easier to fall asleep. We can relax our mind by focusing on pleasant thoughts and experiences when we are trying to fall asleep. Thoughts that bring stress or anxiety keep us awake and make falling asleep more difficult, but peaceful and pleasant thoughts will shorten the time it takes to fall asleep.

We can relax our body and stay still to make it easier to fall asleep. Movement actually stimulates us to wake up and stops the sleep cycle. But getting in a comfortable position and lying still allows us to start our sleep cycle. As we relax our body it becomes easier to relax our mind and to fall asleep. It is my personal belief that one can actually increase their body's ability to renew itself whenever they eventually fall asleep, if they stay in a relaxed state and do not move as they wait to fall asleep.

We need to relax our mind to fall asleep, so removing things that stimulate our mind in our bedroom will help us do that. We can make changes to remove anything that stimulates our mind to stay awake, such as a highly visible clock. We can avoid looking at the clock where we sleep by removing the clock on the wall in our bedroom, or by changing the way our clock on the dresser faces. When we are tempted to look at a clock by simply opening our eyes, then we are stimulating thoughts and anxiety about falling asleep. But by removing clocks from direct view we allow our mind to relax and our thoughts to drift toward pleasant thoughts and to the pleasant dreams of sleep. The same principle applies to any other devices we have, like cell phones and computerized devices, that might make noises or flash lights when we normally sleep. Many electronic devices allow the user to turn off all the bells and whistles daily during the hours a person normally sleeps.

What we eat around our bedtime can also affect our ability to fall asleep. We should be aware of what we consume before we go to sleep as some foods with caffeine, or excessive sugar or carbohydrates, may make it more difficult to fall asleep. Other drinks and foods may make it easier to fall asleep, so we have to search for the foods that work for us. But if we add a natural food or drink that helps us sleep an hour or so before we go to sleep, then this can help improve our ability to fall asleep, and to stay asleep.

What we eat and drink, the exercise we get, and the sleep we get are all related - if we eat right we can exercise better, and if we exercise better we can sleep better. If our health plan includes a plan for these three things then we can improve our health and stay fit.

Now we know how to stay fit and healthy, but what about our happiness. The last chapter is about increasing our happiness for the rest of our life after graduation.

How to Enjoy Life More

Many people are never taught about the importance of happiness, instead they are taught that the focus of life should be being successful at something or accumulating riches, and they are taught that happiness will automatically come when one is successful. Many feel that they must be the best at something like a business, a sport, entertainment, or some profession to be happy. Some will become unbalanced and sacrifice all their time with their family and friends, and even their health in pursuit of success. They believe that having a job title, or a possession, or an award, or a medal will make them happy. But often they find that even when their goal is reached, happiness still stays out of reach.

Does success equal happiness? I would argue they are not at all the same thing, and that *being successful at something does not automatically make one happy*. The truth is that one can be very happy and live a wonderful life without being very rich, or very famous, or without being the very best at something. And likewise one can be very rich, or very famous, or the very best at their profession, but they can still be very unhappy.

After graduation I eventually learned that many of things that others were telling me were so important, were in fact of very little value when it comes to enjoying life. I would argue that it is much better to live a happy life in a small house with an average income, than it is to live sad life in a huge mansion with great riches.

Even though success at different things is a good thing to strive for in a balanced way, it does not guarantee our happiness. The point is that **we must specifically seek the goal of happiness to be able to fully enjoy our life**, regardless of our level of success in life.

But if success alone does not make a person happy, what does? An individual's happiness is a difficult thing to understand, to define, to measure, or to predict. But for a better understanding, and to amuse of any science, psychology, or math fans; I have made an attempt at the impossible. I have attempted to come up with a formula that approximates one's happiness for a period of time. The reason I created this formula is because it gives us a better understanding of the forces that can create or destroy happiness, and it gives us a clue as to how we can enjoy more happiness. Here is my total happiness formula:

$$(P \times PE) - (N \times NE) = TH$$

P = Positive thoughts

PE = Positive Events in life

N = Negative thoughts

NE = Negative Events in life

TH = Total Happiness in a time frame

Happiness is the opposite of sadness, they are in constant conflict with each other, and they detract from each other. In the above formula, when a person has positive thoughts about what they feel is a positive life event it brings them happiness. It also reveals that when a person has negative thoughts on what they feel is a negative life event then it brings them sadness. So simply put our happy thoughts minus or sad thoughts equals how happy or sad we are in a time period.

But a dramatic secret to happiness is revealed in the same formula. Our total happiness depends on our perspective and on what we choose to dwell on. We decide what is considered a positive or negative event, and more importantly we choose which life event we will dwell on. If something we feel is positive or negative happens one day, we may have to think about the event once when it happens, but we normally do not have to continue to dwell on the event throughout the day. The dramatic secret is that we actually have some control over how often and how long we will dwell on each positive or negative life event in our life.

For an example of this let's look at someone who has one positive event and one negative event, and let's assume they feel that both events have approximately the same magnitude of positivity and negativity.

Whether this person is happy this day will depend on what they choose to focus on. The event that they feel is positive that day is the breakfast they just had with their family. The person chooses to think about this positive event ten times that day. They could also feel that they had a negative event the same day of being cut off while driving to work, and then being flipped off by the other driver. But they may choose to only think about this negative event three times the same day. Then their total happiness is greater then their sadness because the 10 times they had positive thoughts on the positive event minus the 3 times they had negative thoughts about the negative event. So looking at the formula they are still plus 7 on the positive side. Which means they are happy this day. The key is that we each get to determine the life events we feel are positive or negative, and more significantly we get to choose how often and how long we will dwell on each life event.

So this shows that **we can actually stack our happiness deck of cards in our favor**

by choosing to dwell more on our positive life events!

In the example above, the person could have been sad all day if they kept thinking, "Why did that person cut me off, and even flip me off today? At first the car driver seemed like a nice old lady, and she even had a cute cuddly little dog with her. I am so upset she flipped me off and then laughed at me just as her little dog barked at me!" Or they could be happy all day thinking of the positive life event of their breakfast with their family. In fact on the same day they could add positive thoughts about an anticipated future positive life events. They could think "I really enjoyed breakfast this morning with my family, I am so lucky to have such a beautiful, funny, and loving family. We always enjoy our time together. And I am really looking forward to the weekend when we go on our family hiking trip!" So while we may have to think of a negative event the day it occurs, we still have the option to think multiple times about the positive events that day, or about positive events in the past, and even about anticipated positive life events in the future.

The formula and this example reveals that we do have some control over our happiness, because we can choose to spend more time thinking about the positive events that occur in our present, past, and future; instead of being continually saddened by dwelling on each negative event that happens to us.

Anyone who just read the first few paragraphs of this chapter now has a powerful secret to instantly increase their total happiness each day for the rest of their life! But there is even more that can be done then just controlling our thoughts to create more happiness in our life.

Now let's look at some **actions** we can take to create more happiness in our life. We have seen that we can boost our happiness by thinking more about the positive events in our life, but now *let's look at **ways to boost our happiness by increasing the number of positive events we have each day in our life!***

We actually have the power to increase our own happiness by taking actions that increase the magnitude and number of positive events in our life! Three actions we can take to do this are: **doing the things we enjoy, creating a happy environment, and spending time with the ones we love.**

Doing the Things We Enjoy

We need to do things we enjoy, or find a way to enjoy the things we already are doing to add happiness to each day. The more time we spend doing the things that bring us joy, the easier it becomes to enjoy each day.

How do we create more positive life events and joy in our lives? The key to maximizing our potential enjoyment of life is by minimizing the time spent doing what we do not like, and by maximizing the time we spend doing the things we love. How can we do this? We may minimize the time we do things that we do not enjoy by becoming more efficient at doing them. If we hate grocery shopping, but someone else in our household loves it, we may have them do more of our shopping. If we hate mowing the lawn, then we may find a more efficient lawnmower that can mow the lawn in much less time. Some things we do not enjoy can be eliminated altogether. If we hate our job, then we may be able to find a job we enjoy, or find a better way to make a living. We can also increase the time we do what we enjoy by planning our activities. If we enjoy going to a sporting event, we can check our work schedule and move our required activities around in order to spend more time enjoying this activity. If we enjoy reading, we may be able to change our schedule and daily activities to allow for more time to read, like reading during our lunch or work breaks, or during a train ride to work. If we enjoy riding a bike, we may be able to ride a bike to work, or to go shopping on some days. The point is that any change that increases the time we spend doing the things that bring us joy, or that decreases the time we spend doing the things that we hate, will increase our total positive life events and our overall happiness in life.

Another way to enjoy what we do is to change our perspective on what we do, whether it is a short term task, or the work we do our entire life. If someone looks at a task they are doing as something that is creating the opportunity for a better future for themselves or for someone they care about, then they are more likely to find joy when they complete the task each day.

If someone has a monotonous task or job, they may make it more interesting and possibly more enjoyable by making a game out of it. For example, if a person works in a call center, they could compete with a like-minded co-worker to see who is the first person to answer a call from a person named "Oscar." Or if they work in sales or in a retail store they could see who is the first to help a customer with the same first name as they have each day. If they have a job assembling products, they could complete with themselves to see if they can match or beat the number of items they assembled the prior day. Or if they made 3 errors in assembling things the day before, they could strive to make 2 or less errors today. One could also create a team competition, or even a business wide competition. There are many ways to spice up our work day when we use our imagination. A job is often what one decides to make it, if we decide to make our job more fun, then we will likely receive more joy from our job.

What can we do about the things we hate doing at work? If there are certain aspects of our work that we do not like, we can reduce the time doing these aspects by doing them more efficiently, or sometimes by partnering with a coworker who enjoys something we do not. For example, if two people work in a restaurant and part of their duties is to mop and sweep the floor each day, but one employee hates mopping the floor and the other employee hates sweeping the floor, then each may partner with the other to do the task they like better more often. Even the individual tasks of our job may be things that we can change, by changing our assigned tasks we can make a job that we have not enjoyed in the past, more fun going forward.

Most people have more leisure time then they spend working, so what we do in our leisure time is a very important part of our life, and of our happiness. Next we will look at some ways to add activities we enjoy to our leisure time.

Many people have activities that they think they would enjoy doing, but they never make the time to do them. If our happiness is important to us, we need to take the time to try some different activities that may appeal to us, and once we find an activity we enjoy we should make time to continually pursue it.

Many people already know an activity they would enjoy doing, but for some reason they keep putting it off. Some people may want to make art, but never make the time to do it. Others may enjoy traveling with family members, but may put off planning their vacation. Others may already know they like hiking, but may never schedule any time to do it. Others may like playing tennis, but keep putting off joining a tennis club or group. And yet others may enjoy sailing, but keep putting it off until they retire. The point is that each day of life is precious, and none of us knows how many days we will get, so we should not put off doing the things we enjoy any longer then necessary. When we stop putting it off and do the things we enjoy we are also filling our life with joy, and when we do the things we enjoy with others then we will sail through life bringing happiness to others too.

One way to choose the enjoyable activities that we will do is to make a few lists. On one list we can put all of the appealing activities that we can think of that are available for us to do. On the second list we can narrow the first list down to all of the enjoyable activities we feel we can currently do. And on the third list we could rank the activities on the second list from what we would enjoy most, to what we would enjoy least. Now we can go down the list starting with the most desirable and enjoyable activities to the least, and we can see which activities we can add to our daily, weekly, and monthly routines. We may be able to add multiple enjoyable activities to our life. But even adding just one enjoyable activity to our life, can bring us much happiness over our entire life.

Now that we understand the importance of what we do, let's take a look at where we do things and how our environment affects our enjoyment of life.

Creating a Happy Environment

The place where we spend time can fill us with joy, or it can make us sad, so to increase our happiness in life we need to look at where we spend time. Nothing is stopping us, we can actually change where we live and work to an environment that inspires happiness. Life is really about how well we play the many different cards we are dealt in our life, in other words making the best of what we have - our situation, possessions, abilities, and our environment - instead of feeling down about something we do not have or something we can not change.

Depending on where we are and what we do, there may be limits to how much we can change our environment. But every change to our environment, even small ones, can make a big difference in our overall long term happiness. A small change in where we work, like a decoration or a plant, can make our work day a little bit more pleasant. Small changes to where we spend time at home can make a huge difference to our overall happiness too because of how much time we spend there. If we add an inspiring picture or piece of art to a room at home where we spend a lot of time, then it may lift our mood many days. We can enjoy each day a little more simply by changing our uncomfortable bed or our couch to something that we truly enjoy sleeping on or sitting on. Each small change can add up to a great long term benefit to our overall happiness. If we open a window in our office, the fresh air may lift our mood. If we open the shades at our home, then the brighter environment may brighten our day.

We can also improve where we spend time by removing clutter and/or organizing our things. Someone can have a beautiful house from the outside, but when you go inside the clutter can make you want to run away. Hoarding is a real problem for many, the problem is that having too many things in one's home or work place actually robs one of their ability to enjoy that space, it steals the ability to do things in the space, and it can also affect one's mental and physical health. But when the clutter is removed and the necessary items are organized, it frees up our living space, it allows us to have more room to move around within the place, and it even frees up space in our minds so we can clearly think and enjoy our life.

We can de-clutter by realistically looking at the items filling up our living space and our work space. If we have not used an item for years, it is unlikely we will ever use it, thus we should consider selling it, giving it away, or even throwing it away especially if it has little or no value. We all have limited space where we live and work, so we should not surround ourselves with excessive clutter. Deciding to keep too much clutter is like being a genie who decides to imprison himself in a small cluttered and uncomfortable lamp, it makes no sense. We can set ourself free from excessive clutter by simply deciding to let our unused items go, and organizing the things we need to keep. Once we let our clutter go then we gain more space in our life to let more joy fit in.

The final way to increase the number of positive events in our life is by spending time with the ones we love.

Spending Time with the Ones We Love

The importance of spending time with the ones we love may seem obvious, but it is not something we are taught in schools. But this is one way to dramatically increase our joy in life.

Spending time with the ones we love can actually improve our lives in many ways, both physically and mentally. Here are some of the benefits:

Reduces stress and anxiety. When we spend time with people we love, we feel supported and accepted. This can help to reduce stress and anxiety, which can have a positive impact on our physical and mental health.

Boosts mood and happiness. Spending time with loved ones can increase levels of oxytocin, a hormone that is associated with feelings of happiness and bonding. This can lead to a more positive outlook on life and a greater sense of well-being.

Improves self-esteem. When we feel loved and supported by our loved ones, it can boost our self-esteem. This is because we feel valued and appreciated, which can lead to a more positive view of ourselves.

Provides a sense of belonging. Spending time with loved ones can help us to feel like we belong. This is because we feel connected to others and part of a community. This can be especially important for people who are feeling lonely or isolated.

Helps to cope with difficult times. When we are going through a difficult time, spending time with loved ones can provide us with support and comfort. They can offer us advice, listen to us vent, or just be there for us. This can help us to cope with difficult times and come out stronger on the other side.

Overall, spending time with the ones we love can have a significant positive impact on our lives. It can reduce stress, boost mood, improve self-esteem, provide a sense of belonging, and help us to cope with difficult times. One outstanding way to improve your life and increase your joy is to make time for the people you love.

But how does one spend more time with the people they love? It is easy, just schedule a fun activity with them. What can you do together? Here are ten ideas of what we can plan to do with others just to get you started:

1. Go on a hike or other outdoor activity

2. Cook a meal together

3. Play games or board games

4. Watch a movie or TV show

5. Go to a concert or sporting event

6. Visit a museum or art gallery

7. Go shopping or window shopping

8. Have a picnic

9. Go for a walk or bike ride

10. Go out to eat together

The possibilities are endless! Just find something that you and your loved ones enjoy doing together.

The point is that happiness is something that we can give ourself. With a little planning and effort we can increase the number of positive events in our life by intentionally doing the things we enjoy, creating a happy environment, and spending more time with the ones we love. And we can also increase our joy each day when we choose to dwell more frequently on the positive events in our life.

Conclusion

So that's it, now you have it! Now you have the additional education you need to ace the after graduation final exam that is called life!

Now you can interview for the job you want, you can perform well in the job you have, you can face workplace politics and bias, you can advance in your career, you can start and grow your own business, you can manage the money you make, you can build strong positive relationships, you can stay fit and healthy, and you also know how to better enjoy life!

I have some final words for you. Please forgive me for throwing one more graduation speech at you, but I will try to keep it short. Here is my "two cents" graduation speech for anyone who will listen.

An education is a wonderful thing, but your education can only open the doors of opportunity for you. You still must choose the door, and walk through it. An education will mean very little to the one that never uses it.

The ones that are going to accomplish great things in life are not necessarily the most educated, but they are the ones who make the most of the education they have, and they are the ones who do not procrastinate!

So please do more then just pat yourself on the back for getting an education, be inspired to take action right away! Go after your dreams and the things you desire!

Start now by making your plan and setting a final goal, then break it down into smaller goals, then create a step by step plan to reach each one of those goals, and keep taking action each day towards your goals until you succeed!

Your education is your tool to build your future, but it only works when you use it! So go now and use it to build a wonderful future for yourself, and for those you care about!

The End

&

The Beginning of Your Life After Graduation!

Enjoy more books by Lee Black in the

"Black Magic Books Series"

INTRODUCTION

Most Effective Natural Treatments for Lupus

When something goes wrong with your immune system, a chronic condition called lupus develops. It loses the ability to tell healthy tissues apart from invaders from outside the body. As a result, your body develops autoimmune bodies that target healthy cells rather than foreign substances. It also results in inflammation, which may impact any area of your body. Notably, every person experiences lupus symptoms differently. A few of the most prevalent symptoms are fever, exhaustion, joint pain, butterfly-shaped rashes, skin lesions, chest pain, shortness of breath, headaches, memory loss, etc.

Although the precise cause of this autoimmune condition is still unknown, doctors think that genetics play a significant part in how it develops. Additionally, there are some things that cause a lupus episode. Some of them include being in the sun, getting sick, taking blood pressure or anti-seizure medications, etc. The disease has a few known risk factors, including your sex, age, and race. Being African-American, Hispanic, or Asian-American, as well as being between the ages of 15 and 45, may increase your risk of developing the condition.

LUPUS MANAGEMENT IN NATURE

In addition to medications, some lifestyle changes can aid in the prevention and management of lupus. Regular exercise, eating well, giving up smoking, etc. are the typical steps that can aid in a more effective treatment of the condition. There are some at-home remedies that can help you live well with lupus in addition to these lifestyle changes.

TURMERIC

Curcumin is a substance that makes turmeric active. This is what makes the effective treatment of autoimmune diseases like lupus possible. This Indian spice also has anti-inflammatory qualities that are beneficial in easing symptoms like joint pain, rashes, etc. You can include turmeric in your regular diet to use it in this way.

Adding turmeric to milk is another way to consume it.

Check to see if the milk you're drinking is hot.

The taste of the milk can also be improved by adding honey. Turmeric may not be appropriate for you if you also have gallbladder issues. Therefore, before using it for lupus, it is always advisable to consult your doctor.

GINGER

Lupus is one of many illnesses and conditions for which ginger is thought to be an effective ingredient. It helps to lessen joint pain and swelling because of its anti-inflammatory and antioxidant properties. There are many ways you can incorporate ginger into your diet. Making ginger tea is one method. Ginger juice is another ingredient that you can add to produce. Consult your physician to find out the precise dosage of ginger you should use.

Alcohol from apple cider

According to medical professionals, hydrochloric acid, which can be added to your body by using apple cider vinegar, is a nutrient that lupus patients lack. It might increase the amount of hydrochloric acid your body produces. It enhances nutrient absorption in the body and aids in detoxification as well. You can use apple cider vinegar for this by mixing a teaspoon of the substance with a glass of warm water. Add some lemon juice to this beverage and consume it three times per day. Make sure to consume it 20 minutes before eating.

VIRGIN COCONUT OIL

Coconut oil, one of the healthiest oils, may be able to assist you in reducing the adverse effects that your body's defense system may have on you. Additionally, it may help with digestion, blood sugar, and cholesterol regulation, and it may also be effective. You can cook with coconut oil. Be aware of the portions.

SALT OF EPSOM

The use of an Epsom salt bath can help relieve fatigue, which is one of the most prevalent signs and symptoms of lupus. It is well known that this salt helps the body better absorb magnesium. Additionally, it aids in the removal of harmful substances from the body and lessens joint pain and inflammation. You simply need to add a cup of Epsom salt to your bathwater and stir it thoroughly to prepare an Epsom salt bath. Then, for relief, take a 15-minute soak in this water.

Notably, those with diabetes or kidney disease should avoid this.

Basil

One of the main factors that causes lupus flare-ups is stress. You can use basil to manage your body's reaction to stress. It is a herb that is bursting with anti-inflammatory and antioxidant properties. It is also referred to as Tulsi and helps with organ function and fatigue relief. The cultivation of well-being is another benefit of tulsi. You can chew a few basil leaves every day to use it for this. Basil can also be used to make herbal tea, which you can drink twice or three times per day.

TOP 10 WONDERFUL HOME TREATMENTS FOR LUPUS

An inflammation of the skin, heart, joints, lungs, kidneys, liver, nerves, and blood vessels is a common symptom of lupus, a chronic autoimmune disease in which the immune system attacks the connective tissues of the body. Lupus can be brought on by genetics, the environment, sunlight, specific medications, and persistent infections. Numerous symptoms, including exhaustion, swelling, pain in the muscles and joints, low-grade fever, chest pain, enlargement of the lymph nodes, shortness of breath, headaches, fluid retention, and photosensitivity, can be brought on by this condition. Some people who have lupus may also develop potentially fatal complications like kidney issues or cardiovascular disease. Several home remedies for lupus are natural and you can try them. This condition can be avoided by using these treatments.

1. REMEDY USING APPLE CIDER VINEGAR

There is frequently insufficient hydrochloric acid in lupus patients. ACV (apple cider vinegar) has the power to boost the body's production of hydrochloric acid. It also enhances nutrient absorption and facilitates detoxification in general.

Take 1 teaspoon of raw, unfiltered ACV and mix it with 1 glass of warm water to make the remedy. You can add some lemon juice to increase the effectiveness of thetreatment. Then, drink this mixture twice or three times per day, about 20 minutes before eating.

2. EMPLOY EPSOM SALT

An Epsom salt bath can help with fatigue, a common lupus symptom. It also aids in reducing joint pain and inflammation. In addition, it facilitates the body's removal of toxins and aids in the absorption of magnesium.

Take one cup of Epsom salt and stir it into one bathtub of warm water for this treatment. Next, spend 15 to 20 minutes soaking in this solution. Follow this advice several times a week for quick results. This remedy should not be used if you have diabetes or kidney issues.

3. TREATMENT FOR LUPUS WITH COCONUT OIL

Numerous hair care products contain the well-known ingredient coconut oil. Due to its medium-chain fatty acids, it also assists in regulating immunity and reducing adverse immune reactions. Furthermore, this oil has a host of health advantages, including improved digestion, cholesterol reduction, blood sugar regulation, and treatment of candida infection.

You can consume 2 tablespoons of virgin coconut oil daily for this reason.

Cooking with coconut oil is an option.

You can also incorporate this oil into your drinks and smoothies. Observe moderation when using this oil.

4. HOLY BASIL CURE

Holy basil can help you control how you react to the stress that causes lupus. In addition, it can improve overall wellbeing, reduce fatigue, and control organ function. Holy basil also has antioxidant and anti-inflammatory properties. Every day, you can chew on some basil leaves.

As an alternative, steep some fresh basil leaves or 1 teaspoon of dried basil for five to ten minutes in 1 cup of hot water. Then strain it and add some honey to make it sweet. This herbal tea that results should be drank daily in two to three cups.

5. UTILIZE TURMERIC

A 2012 study in the Journal of Renal Nutrition found that turmeric can reduce proteinuria, systolic blood pressure, and hematuria in people with refractory lupus nephritis. Curcumin, an ingredient in this spice, prevents and treats inflammatory autoimmune diseases like lupus.

To accomplish this, mix one cup of milk with one teaspoon of turmeric powder. This mixture will later be cooked and sweetened with some raw honey. After that, sip a cup of milk with turmeric once or twice daily. You can also consume supplements of turmeric. Consult your doctor for advice on dosage. Turmeric should not be used by those with gallbladder issues.

6. GINGER AS A LUPUS TREATMENT

Ginger can typically treat lupus symptoms associated with arthritis. As a result of its strong anti-inflammatory and antioxidant properties, it can reduce lupus-related swelling and joint pain.

Ginger should be used in your cooking. You could also juice a piece of fresh ginger root that is 1 inch long. Add it later to freshly squeezed vegetable and fruit juices. Remember to talk to your doctor about the appropriate dosage and suitability before taking any supplements that contain ginger.

7. THE OMEGA-3 FATTY ACIDS

Due to their anti-inflammatory properties, omega-3 fatty acids, which contain eicosapentaenoic acid, can help to reduce the symptoms of lupus. Additionally, it can enhance blood flow and blood vessel performance. This demonstrates that fish oil has the ability to counteract potential cardioprotective effects.

It is permissible to incorporate into one's diet foods that contain high levels of Omega-3 Fatty Acids. Some of the best foods high in omega-3 fatty acids include walnuts, chia seeds, ground flaxseeds, salmon, mackerel, sardines, tuna, and herring. You can also take supplements that contain fish oil.

The right dosage should be discussed with your doctor.

8. EXERCISE

Since exercise is so important for enhancing health, daily, moderate exercise helps prevent fatigue and joint stiffness. Exercise is also very helpful for minimizing the side effects of steroids and other medications prescribed to treat lupus.

Last but not least, exercise enhances life quality and elevates mood. Every day, it's a good idea to engage in low-impact activities like swimming, walking, cycling, stretching, Tai-Chi, water aerobics, or low-impact aerobics. It's unlikely that they'll exert pressure on your joints.

9. UTILIZE CARROTS

Carrots contain anti-inflammatory compounds that lessen lupus. The vitamin A content of carrots is also high. Eating carrots can help with mouth sores, lethargy, dizziness, depression, and joint pain.

You should include carrot juice in your daily diet for this reason. For the best and fastest results, drink this juice two to three times daily.

10. VITAMIN D

Basically, autoimmune conditions like multiple sclerosis, rheumatoid arthritis, and lupus have been linked to low vitamin D3 levels. Consuming foods high in vitamin D, such as cheese, egg yolks, tofu, mushrooms, salmon, and other fatty fish, should help you get enough vitamin D in your diet.

How to Naturally Cure Lupus

An autoimmune condition called lupus has the potential to affect numerous bodily systems.

1 Immune system-suppressing drugs are used to treat lupus in conventional medicine.

19

You can treat lupus with functional medicine by boosting your immune system and getting it back to working at its best.

Lupus and other autoimmune diseases are not considered immune system diseases by conventional medicine. Instead, they inform you that it is genetically determined and that your only course of action is to manage your symptoms for the rest of your life.

Your risk of developing an autoimmune disease does in fact have a genetic component. As a result of leaky gut, food sensitivities, toxins, infections, stress, or a combination of these factors, the environment is the greater threat to your health.

You can cure lupus and eliminate your pain by addressing its underlying causes. Later, I'll explain my tried-and-true method for tackling your chronic illness's underlying cause. Let's explore lupus more.

WHAT DEFINES LUPUS?

The immune system's inability to effectively distinguish between foreign material and healthy tissue leads to lupus. Most autoimmune illnesses only impact one particular system. Rheumatoid arthritis, for instance, affects the joints, and multiple sclerosis, the brain and spinal cord. Lupus, on the other hand, simultaneously affects multiple systems.

All autoimmune diseases are comparable in that they are an immune system reaction brought on by systemic inflammation that causes your body to attack itself, regardless of what organ or system is attacked. There are five underlying factors that contribute to the development of lupus.

5 FUNDAMENTAL ROOT CAUSES OF LUPUS

The root cause of autoimmunity consists of five factors and starts in the gut.

Your gut is the doorway to health, I say all the time.

Your skin, your brain, and your immune system are just a few of the many areas of your health that are influenced by the condition of your gut. A healthy immune system is impossible if your gut is unhealthy. After all, your gut is home to 80% of your immune system.

1. LEAKY STOMACH

The tight junctions that hold your intestinal wall together become loose, which results in leaky gut. The lining of your stomach can be compared to a drawbridge. The bridge is no match for the tiniest boats (micronutrients in food). This essential system enables the bloodstream to absorb important nutrients from your food.

All of these particles are identified by your immune system as foreign invaders when you have a leaky gut, which puts your immune system on high alert and causes a significant increase in inflammation to combat these free radicals. Your immune system eventually becomes out of control as a result of this ongoing stress and starts unintentionally attacking your own tissues. As a result, one of the most frequent causes of autoimmune disease is leaky gut. Therefore, you need to fix your leaky gut if you want to reverse lupus.

2. GLUTEN

A protein called gluten that is present in wheat and other grains is now virtually ubiquitous in our modern world and has been linked to more than 55 diseases. It is present in more than just bread and pasta, which are both made of flour. It is used as a filler in supplements, medications, and meat substitutes. Furthermore, cross-contamination can result in "gluten-free" foods containing gluten, as is the case with body products like toothpaste.

Because it causes the release of zonulin, a chemical that instructs your gut lining to "open up," in your intestines, gluten is the leading cause of leaky gut. It can stress your immune system because it is also very inflammatory.

The chemical structure of the gluten protein is similar to that of some of your body's tissues, particularly your thyroid, which can cause molecular mimicry, in which your body mistakenly attacks your tissues for gluten.

It is advised to cut gluten out of your diet, particularly if you have a gluten sensitivity. It is advised to eliminate diet to determine if you have a gluten sensitivity.

3. TOXINS

The main toxins observed in people with autoimmune diseases are toxic molds (mycotoxins) and heavy metals like mercury. Mycotoxins, which are volatile substances made by toxic molds and found naturally in our food and cleaning supplies, severely compromise the immune system.

Our bodies' reactions to toxins are intricately layered. After all, there are thousands of chemicals, and we're only now starting to understand how they affect the body, not to mention how they interact with one another. There are several hypotheses as to why having a high toxic burden increases your risk of developing an autoimmune disease.

One theory is that some toxins, especially heavy metals, cause actual tissue damage. These damaged cells are no longer recognized by your immune system as being a part of your body, leading it to attack them under the pretext that they are foreign invaders.

An additional hypothesis holds that the immune system's inflammatory response to the harm caused by toxins causes the damage. The immune system goes into overdrive as a result of the chronic exposure, attacking everything—including healthy tissues.

It may seem overwhelming, but it doesn't have to be. By consuming organic foods, employing non-toxic cleaning and beauty products, and engaging in regular detoxification, you can manage your toxins. Glutathione is the primary detoxifying agent in your body, so I advise taking extra supplements of it.

4. INFECTIONS

Infections caused by bacteria, viruses, and other toxins have long been thought to play a role in the development of autoimmune disease. Epstein-Barr (the monovirus), Herpes Simplex 1 and 2, and E are a few infections that have ties to autoimmunity. coli.

Epstein-Barr and herpes simplex viruses remain in your system forever. But if your immune system is strong, you can keep them under control. Stress or illness can weaken your immune system, allowing the infection to reactivate. 4.

Once the virus is active, the immune system's inflammatory response causes tissue damage, which leads to more inflammation and a stronger immune response. This ongoing inflammation leads to the development of an autoimmune disease. To reverse your autoimmune disease, you must treat your infections.

5. STRESS

Our bodies can withstand severe stress by design. This is stress brought on by a protracted meeting, a phone call with an ex-spouse, being stuck in traffic, etc. You stop experiencing the effects of stress once the stressor is gone. However, if your stress response is constantly active, your immune system will remain on high alert, which will cause it to go rogue and start attacking everything in sight.

For effective stress management, adaptogens must be taken to support a healthy stress response. Additionally, for the best stress response, learning natural stress relief techniques is crucial.

UTILIZING THE MYERS WAY, REVERSE LUPUS

The Myers Way is an effective treatment for chronic illness that targets the underlying causes of symptoms. To address the underlying causes of autoimmune disease and help you reverse your condition and live a full, symptom-free life, this way of living is based on four pillars.

Heal Your Gut is Pillar one

The gut needs to be healed first. In functional medicine, we employ the successful 4R strategy:.

Eliminate the bad - Get rid of anything that has an adverse effect on the environment of your gastrointestinal tracts, including toxins, inflammatory foods, and intestinal infections like SIBO and yeast overgrowth. .

Restore what's been lost by including HCL and digestive enzymes in your daily routine to support digestion and nutrient absorption.

Reinoculate with healthy bacteria — Restore beneficial bacteria with a probiotic supplement to re-establish a healthy balance of bacteria that will heal your gut.

Gut repair: Give the body the nutrients it needs to help the gut mend itself. Your immune system and intestinal lining are supported by Leaky Gut Revive Max. It now comes in three flavors to suit various palates. Your gut will also heal as a result of consuming bone broth or adding collagen protein.

ABOLISH GLUTEN, GRAINS, AND LEGUMES, THE SECOND PILLAR

It's time to change your diet after your gut has healed. Eliminate foods that harm your intestinal tract and cause inflammation, such as gluten, grains, and legumes, as a starting point. The nightshade family of vegetables, which includes peppers, tomatoes, and potatoes, should be avoided by people who have autoimmune diseases. These plants contain a lot of lectins, which harm the gut lining, quickly enter the bloodstream, and do not degrade when cooked.

TAME THE TOXINS IS PILLAR THREE

After taking care of the first two pillars, many patients experience improvement. If you do not notice improvement, you might expose yourself to too many toxins. Every day, thousands of toxins are presented to us. They are present in the food you eat, the cookware you use, the air you breathe, the water you drink, and the cosmetics you use.

Unfortunately, it is impossible for you to completely avoid toxins. Decrease your body's toxic load by doing the following.

purchasing healthy body and skincare products.

Get a HEPA filter for your home to purify the air. Air, Doctorair filters can be used

Whenever possible, purchase healthy food and consume organic food. Purchase at least free-range chicken, grass-fed beef, and wild-caught seafood because these items can be pricey.

Install water filters on your shower faucets and sinks to purify the water.

HEAL YOUR INFECTIONS AND REDUCE YOUR STRESS, THE FOURTH PILLAR

It's time to look further if your symptoms haven't disappeared after dealing with the first three pillars. Healing infections and reducing stress are the main goals of The Myers Way's fourth pillar.

It is advise implementing daily stress-relieving practices to reduce stress. Breathing exercises, music, dancing, long walks, and yoga etc.

Adding Adrenal Support to promote healthy energy levels and ideal adrenal gland health. Adrenal Support uses an innovative blend of adaptogenic herbs to encourage a more balanced physical and emotional stress response.

Let's discuss the signs and how lupus is identified now that you are aware of the causes of the disease and how The Myers Way can help you naturally reverse it.

MANIFESTATIONS OF LUPUS

Lupus symptoms and signs
As previously stated, lupus, also referred to as systemic lupus erythematosus (SLE), can affect different body parts. Its symptoms and signs can differ from person to person and between men and women. Here are the symptoms of lupus in both men and women.

SYMPTOMS OF LUPUS IN FEMALES

Women are more likely than men to develop lupus, especially those who are childbearing age. In actuality, lupus affects 90% of women. The following are the most typical signs and symptoms of lupus in females.

Extreme tiredness that does not go away with rest is referred to as fatigue.

Joint stiffness and pain: Joint stiffness and pain, especially in the morning.

Skin rashes, including those that take the form of a butterfly across the cheeks and nose or other rashes that get worse when exposed to the sun.

Fever: A temperature greater than 100.05°F that develops for no apparent reason.

Fingers or toes that turn white or blue in response to cold or stress are known as Raynaud's phenomenon.

Breathing problems, chest pain, or a cough can all be symptoms of shortness of breath.

Blood or protein in the urine or leg swelling are symptoms of kidney problems.

Sores in the mouth or nose that last longer than a week are referred to as mouth sores.

Hair loss: Hair that sheds in clumps or in patches.

Chronic headaches that are frequently accompanied by light or sound sensitivity.

Along with these signs and symptoms, women with lupus may also have irregular menstrual cycles, such as heavier or more painful periods or periods that stop entirely. Preeclampsia and preterm delivery are two complications that are more likely to occur in pregnant lupus patients.

It's important to remember that not all lupus-affected women will experience these symptoms, and some may experience other symptoms not included in the above list.

MEN WITH LUPUS: SYMPTOMS

Men are less likely to develop lupus. Lupus symptoms are similar in men and women, but they can also include erectile dysfunction and decreased sex drive. Men with lupus may also be more prone to certain complications, like cardiovascular disease and kidney disease.

Due to frequent misdiagnosis or neglect, lupus diagnosis is difficult to obtain. Your functional medicine physician can request a number of tests to determine whether you have lupus. .

HOW IS LUPUS RECOGNIZED?

A doctor will typically review your medical history, as well as any family history, and look for any indications of inflammation. Lupus cannot be diagnosed with a single test because many different factors must cohere, and the process can take years. One of the biggest grievances most lupus sufferers have is this.

Examining your medical history, having your urine tested to see if there is protein or blood in it, and having a physical examination to check for skin rashes and tender joints are among the most frequent tests.

Blood tests can be used to identify particular antibodies and other inflammation markers that are frequently present in lupus patients, such as antinuclear antibodies (ANA), anti-dsDNA antibodies, and anti-Smith antibodies.

In order to check for organ damage brought on by lupus, such as damage to the heart or lungs, imaging studies like X-rays, ultrasounds, or CT scans may be prescribed.

For lupus to be identified, at least four symptoms must be present. Additionally, the symptoms must be persistent and unrelated to any other medical condition.

CURE FOR LUPUS

Whether you have lupus, rheumatoid arthritis, Hashimoto's, or another autoimmune disorder, you can manage your symptoms, regain your energy, and feel like yourself once more. The Myers Way Autoimmune Kit combines four of the most crucial dietary supplements for anyone worried about autoimmunity for complete support.

The four supplements are as follows

Each lozenge of resveratrol provides the health advantages of 2-4 glasses of red wine without the added sugar, alcohol, or risk of yeast overgrowth. In addition to fighting free radicals very effectively, resveratrol also reduces inflammation.

L-glutamine is a necessary amino acid that aids in preserving a healthy intestinal barrier and reduces sugar cravings.

The body's most effective detoxifier and free radical scavenger is glutathione, which is essential for a healthy immune system and toxin removal.

Curcumin Super Soluble: This fat-soluble formulation was created by my doctor to support a healthy immune system and inflammatory response.

ADVICE ON CURING LUPUS

Chronic autoimmune disease lupus can be extremely painful and inflamed.

Although there is no known treatment for this condition, medication and lifestyle changes can help manage symptoms.

Clinical trials have shown that medical marijuana is a promising treatment for typical lupus symptoms. It is both safe and effective. The drug may treat a variety of issues, including pain and mood.

The anti-inflammatory properties of a CBD and THC mixture make it a potential candidate for lupus treatment.

A natural cure for lupus is not meant to take the place of medication. Always seek professional advice before attempting any of these home remedies.

Systemic lupus erythematosus (SLE), also known as lupus, is a long-term autoimmune condition. The skin, joints, kidneys, and brain are just a few of the body organs and tissues that it may impact.

These body parts become inflamed as a result of lupus, which makes sufferers feel pain and discomfort. Among the lupus symptoms are:.

- fatigue that is persistent.
- chills and fever.
- lesions or skin rashes.
- joint and muscle pain in muscles.
- thermal flashes.

Sadly, there is no treatment for the condition. medicine (e.g.   , hydroxychloroquine, corticosteroids, and retinoids) are employed to treat the symptoms of lupus.

People with lupus can, however, combine prescription medication with a few complementary therapies. When it comes to managing symptoms, incorporating natural lupus herbs into your daily routine could be a game changer.

The ten various herbs and supplements that can be beneficial additions to your lupus management strategy are discussed in this guide.

1. CANNABIS USED FOR MEDICAL PURPOSES

It has been discovered that cannabinoids, which are present in medical cannabis, may have therapeutic value for lupus sufferers. Cannabis may ease a variety of lupus symptoms and enhance general health.

better sleep and pain relief.

Many lupus patients report having chronic pain as a symptom.

This may have a significant effect on their standard of living.

Neuropathic and inflammatory pain are just two of the many types of pain that medical cannabis may help with.

49

Additionally, medical marijuana may enhance the quality of sleep.

Due to pain or other symptoms, lupus patients frequently experience disturbed sleep. Patients who take cannabis medicine may experience longer periods of deep, restorative sleep.

EFFECTS THAT REDUCE INFLAMMATION

Lupus is characterized by chronic inflammation, which can harm tissues and organs. Tetrahydrocannabinol (THC) and cannabidiol (CBD), the two main cannabis cannabinoids, are known for their ability to reduce inflammation. Medical marijuana may help relieve lupus-related symptoms by lowering inflammation and may even slow the development of the condition.

According to a 2021 study that was published in Cannabis and Cannabinoid Research, the combination of CBD and THC has anti-inflammatory properties. Inflammation levels may be decreased by CBD therapy alone. THC does not, however, by itself lessen inflammation.

QUALITY OF LIFE AND EMOTIONAL HEALTH

Physically and emotionally, having lupus can be difficult. It has been demonstrated that medical marijuana improves mood. In fact, treating mood disorders with cannabis is one of its uses that has the most clinical evidence behind it.

Cannabinoids may be helpful for lupus patients who struggle with anxiety and depression. Medical cannabis may enhance quality of life by addressing these psychological effects of lupus.

1. "GREEN TEA."

Antioxidants known as polyphenols, more specifically catechins, are abundant in green tea. The most prevalent catechine, epigallocatechin-3-gallate (EGCG), has been investigated for its anti-inflammatory properties.

According to a 2018 study that was published in the International Journal of

Environmental Research, EGCG has anti-inflammatory and immunomodulatory properties. The substance also has antioxidant properties that might be helpful for treating autoimmune diseases.

These antioxidant qualities can control the immune system in lupus sufferers. Green tea may, in fact, lessen lupus activity and possibly enhance general health.

Lupus can cause stress that affects both the mind and the body. L-theanine, an amino acid found in green tea, helps people relax by boosting the generation of alpha brain waves. Stress and anxiety may be lessened by this calming effect.

2. LACTOBACILLUS

The genus of helpful bacteria called Lactobacillus, which is found in the gut, is essential for preserving gut health. Maintaining a healthy gut microbiota has become more evident in recent research.

The intricate community of microbes in the digestive tract is known as the gut microbiome. It is essential for proper digestion, nutrient absorption, and immune system operation. Several autoimmune diseases, including lupus, have been linked to dysbiosis, an imbalance of gut bacteria.

Probiotics are beneficial bacteria, including Lactobacillus strains. They may help maintain a balanced gut microbiome, resulting in an immune system that is in good shape.

Additionally demonstrated to have anti-inflammatory properties are Lactobacillus strains. One strain may help lower the production of proteins linked to the onset of lupus,

Think about the following possibilities to include this herbal treatment for lupus in your regular routine:.

Consume fermented foods: Include lactobacillus-rich fermented foods in your diet, such as yoghurt, kefir, sauerkraut, kimchi, and kombucha.

Purchase probiotic supplements: Opt for ones that contain different Lactobacillus strains and are of high quality. The best dosage to take and any possible drug interactions should be discussed with your doctor.

Keep up a healthy diet: Eat a diet high in fruits, vegetables, whole grains, lean proteins, and healthy fats to support a healthy gut microbiome.

Steer clear of processed foods and excessive sugar.

3. OMEGA-3 FATTY ACIDS

Eicosapentaenoic acid (EPA) and docosahexaenoic acid (DHA), two omega-3 fatty acids renowned for their powerful anti-inflammatory properties, are abundant in fish oil. For people with lupus, immune regulation is crucial. Fish oil supplements may lessen the disease activity associated with lupus by assisting in the immune response's balancing.

A randomized, controlled trial that was published in The Journal of Rheumatology found that giving patients fish oil improved their skin conditions. In this placebo-controlled trial, the scientists discovered that those who took fish oil had fewer lupus symptoms.

The overall quality of life among lupus patients was positively impacted by fish oil, according to results of another randomised trial from 2015 that was published in Nutrition Journal. 50 patients participated in the study, with half receiving a placebo and the other half receiving doses of fish oil supplements.

The group receiving treatment reported greater health improvement at the conclusion of the six-month trial period.

Fish that are fatty (e.g.), mackerel, salmon, and tuna) are great sources of omega-3 fatty acids. For those who are unable to consume fish, there are natural lupus supplements such as fish oil capsules.

4. ST. THE JOHN'S WORT

A well-liked herbal supplement called John's wort (Hypericum perforatum) may be helpful in treating anxiety and mild to moderate depression. The herb may influence a lupus patient's immune system while also improving mood.

A substance derived from St. Anti-inflammatory properties can be found in John's wort. Astilbin treatment in mice resulted in a decrease in the amount of inflammatory compounds found in their blood serum, according to a 2015 study. The herbal compound, based on the findings, slows the progression of lupus by lowering autoimmune cell activity.

5. PEONY IN WHITE

Paeonia lactiflora, a traditional Chinese medicinal herb, has been used for many years to treat a variety of illnesses. Thanks to an active ingredient known as paeoniflorin, modern research has started to look into the potential advantages of white peony for people with lupus.

Paeoniflorin has shown immunomodulatory effects. The substance suppressed the activity of immune cells in mouse models, according to a study published in the year 2021's International Immunopharmacology. These results imply that the drug can be used to treat inflammatory cell-mediated diseases like lupus.

6. VITAMIN D

According to research, vitamin D has immunomodulatory properties that may help control the immune system's operation. Vitamin D may assist in reducing lupus-related inflammation, which may result in a decline in disease activity.

Osteoporosis prevention is another advantage of vitamin D for people with lupus. Osteoporosis, which is characterized by fragile and brittle bones, is more likely to occur in people with lupus.

Low vitamin D levels have been associated with a heightened risk of cardiovascular disease and a weakened resistance to infections. A higher risk of these complications already exists in lupus sufferers. Achieving adequate vitamin D levels can improve general health and wellbeing.

To make sure you get enough vitamin D, try to strike a healthy balance between getting enough sun exposure, eating a healthy diet, and taking supplements. You can access this all-natural lupus treatment in this way.

Lupus sufferers should exercise caution, though, as exposure to UV rays can result in flare-ups. It's crucial to go over safe sun exposure techniques with your doctor.

NAC is short for N-Acetyl Cysteine.

In a 2021 study, female mice were used to examine how the gut microbiome affected the development of lupus. The results of the study demonstrated a significant relationship between microbiome composition and function and the severity of autoimmune diseases.

In the same study, the researchers found that N-acetyl cysteine (NAC) treatment led to better balance in the gut microbiome. N-acetyl cysteine is a naturally occurring amino acid used as a supplement for its antioxidant and anti-inflammatory properties.

Improved gut barrier performance and a reduction in inflammatory responses are both associated with a more balanced gut microbiota. Moreover, NAC treatment was also associated with reduced levels of inflammatory cytokines and increased blood antioxidant capacity.

Eating foods high in the protein cysteine is essential if you want to increase the amount of NAC in your management plan.

Sunflower seeds, legumes, chicken, and turkey are a few examples of such foods. A supplement form of NAC is also offered.

7. CURCUMIN, OR TURMERIC

Curcumin, a potent anti-inflammatory and antioxidant, is the turmeric compound that is active. It has been demonstrated to be effective against autoimmune diseases in a number of preclinical and clinical studies.

Curcumin lowers proteinuria (high levels of protein in the urine), which is one of the early symptoms of lupus, as well as renal inflammation, according to a 2019 study published in the journal International Immunopharmacology. Curcumin may be helpful in treating skin lesions, the researchers added.

Consuming curcumin reduced the binding of autoantibodies, according to another study that was published in Molecular Nutrition and Food Research. These antibodies target the body's own tissue. This study found that curcumin prevented autoantibodies from binding to the body's own cells, which could help prevent inflammation and tissue damage in lupus patients.

The best way to incorporate turmeric for lupus into one's diet is to take it in supplement form. Curcumin capsules have high bioavailability, meaning the body readily absorbs the medicine.

8. PEPPERMINT

Peppermint has been traditionally used for its various health benefits. It's been used to relieve gastrointestinal issues, reduce inflammation and ease headaches. For individuals with lupus, incorporating peppermint into their daily routine might relieve certain symptoms.

Lupus can sometimes lead to gastrointestinal symptoms, such as bloating, indigestion and abdominal pain. Peppermint tea can help ease these symptoms by calming the smooth muscles in the digestive tract.

Peppermint essential oils for lupus have analgesic properties and can help alleviate pain when applied to the skin. However, it's essential to perform a patch test before applying peppermint essential oil, as it can cause skin irritation.

Peppermint contains piperine, a component that's been shown to inhibit the pro-inflammatory response in cells. This means peppermint may help relieve joint pain and other symptoms associated with lupus flares.

WHAT IS LUPUS TREATMENT?

Lupus treatment is the best way to manage your symptoms, feel better, and keep the disease from getting worse.

Treatment for lupus -- also known as systemic lupus erythematosus (SLE) --

depends on your symptoms and how severe they are. You may benefit from treatment:.

- Ease your symptoms.
- Bring down inflammation.
- Prevent and relieve flares.
- Prevent organ damage and other health problems.
- Medications for Lupus.
- inflammatory drugs.

If you have lupus, you may have joint pain and swelling, especially in your fingers, wrists, or knees. Sometimes, you may have a fever. Nonsteroidal anti-inflammatory drugs (NSAIDs) can usually help with these problems. You can buy them without a prescription.

The following are examples of over-the-counter anti-inflammatory medications:.

- Acetaminophen.
- Aspirin.
- Ibuprofen.
- Naproxen.

SIDE EFFECTS OF ANTI-INFLAMMATORY DRUGS

Sometimes, anti-inflammatories can irritate your stomach, so take them with food or milk. NSAIDs, especially at higher doses, raise your chances of a heart attack or stroke.

anti-malarial medicines

There are some drugs that can treat both lupus and malaria. They might provide relief for joint pain, mouth sores, and skin rashes. They might also reduce your risk of blood clots, which some lupus sufferers worry about.

Antimalarial medications shield your skin from ultraviolet sunlight damage and may shield your body from organ damage associated with lupus.

anti-malarial medication side effects.

Side effects like stomach upset are typically rare and minor.

CORTICOSTEROIDS

Your immune system mistakenly attacks healthy tissue because of the overactive immune system that lupus causes. The immune response is compromised by corticosteroids. If lupus causes issues with your blood vessels, kidneys, brain, or heart, your doctor might advise taking them.

Corticosteroids, taken orally or intravenously, quickly reduce swelling, warmth, and pain in joints brought on by inflammation. They can also stop long-term organ damage.

CORTICOSTEROID SIDE EFFECTS

Serious negative side effects of corticosteroids include:.

- increased risk of infection.
- damaged or brittle bones, particularly in the hips.
- weakness of the muscles.
- Diabetes.
- Cataracts.

Additionally, you might experience mood swings, weight gain, and bloating. If your symptoms disappear temporarily, your doctor will likely prescribe the lowest dose they can and taper it off.

Medications that suppress the immune system

Similar to corticosteroids, these medications weaken your immune system, control symptoms, and aid in preventing long-term organ damage. In the event that corticosteroids have not relieved your symptoms, your doctor may prescribe them.

There are several typical immunosuppressive medications for lupus.

- Imuran, or azathioprine.
- Cytoxan (cyclophosphamide).
- Methotrexate, also known as Rheumatrex.

In some circumstances, corticosteroids and immunosuppressive medications may be combined. By doing so, you'll be using less of each type of medication, potentially lowering any side effects.

You and your doctor should compare the potential side effects of both types of medications to how well they reduce your lupus symptoms.

IMMUNOSUPPRESSIVE DRUG SIDE EFFECTS

The adverse effects of immunosuppressive medications can be very bad. For instance, they may make it more difficult for your body to fight infections and increase your risk of developing certain cancers.

A type of hepatitis or pancreatitis are two azathioprine side effects.

Cyclophosphamide may cause issues with the bladder, hair, or fertility.

Sun sensitivity, mouth sores, liver damage, lung infections, nausea, headaches, and liver problems are just a few side effects of methotrexate.

additional pharmaceuticals

The following classes of medication may also be recommended by your doctor:

Anticoagulants. These thin your blood to stop clots, a potentially fatal lupus symptom.

The monoclonal antibodies. The initial medication made specifically to treat lupus is belimumab (Benlysta). It is administered subcutaneously (under the skin) or intravenously (in a vein) and targets particular immune cells. It might lessen your need for steroid therapy, but it hasn't been thoroughly investigated for the most severe lupus types. Another monoclonal antibody called Rituxan (Rituximab) has the potential to treat lupus when other therapies have failed. Adults with moderate to severe SLE who are taking other lupus medications are treated with anifrolumab-fnia (Saphnelo).

injection of corticotropin into the repository.

A medication known as H.P.

Your body may be able to produce cortisol and other steroid hormones to fight inflammation with the aid of Acthar Gel.

adverse effects of other drugs.

Anticoagulants frequently cause bloating, diarrhea, upset stomach, vomiting, and appetite loss as side effects. Rarely, symptoms like bruising, a skin rash, a sore throat, back pain, or jaundice—yellow skin and eyes—may appear.

Monoclonal antibodies may result in issues like headaches, nausea, hives, or changes in blood pressure.

Over time, these typically disappear.

Acthar Gel has the potential to result in swelling, adjustments to blood pressure or glucose tolerance, changes in mood or appetite, and weight gain.

LUPUS ALTERNATIVE THERAPIES

Anything you use as a form of treatment in place of conventional medicine is considered alternative medicine. Some lupus sufferers make an effort to reduce their symptoms by:

- Acupuncture.
- Biofeedback.
- Massage.
- Meditation.

- Chiropractic procedures.

HERBS AND OTHER DIETARY SUPPLEMENTS

These remedies do not work in place of medical care, according to studies. In fact, some supplements may exacerbate your lupus symptoms.

However, some studies have shown that when used in conjunction with conventional treatments, acupuncture, meditation, and biofeedback can reduce pain and stress. Complementary medicine refers to this.

Before attempting any complementary or alternative lupus treatments, consult your doctor.

LIFESTYLE MODIFICATIONS

You'll feel better and avoid flare-ups with a healthy lifestyle. Along with preventing kidney disease, heart attacks, and strokes, it can also help with other lupus-related conditions.

Consider the following advice

- Consume a diet that is balanced.

- To protect your heart and blood vessels, stop smoking (or refrain from starting).

- Rest well to lessen fatigue, a typical lupus symptom.

- To improve mood, sleep, and heart health, exercise on a daily basis.

- Sunscreen should always be worn outside.

- To protect yourself from infections, get the flu and pneumonia vaccines.

PHARMACEUTICALS AND TREATMENTS FOR LUPUS

When is lupus discovered?

Lupus develops when the immune system of the body malfunctions and attacks normal tissues and organs. The majority of medical professionals agree that genetics, hormones, or external triggers like medications or infections are the most common causes of lupus. Lupus can be brought on by a variety of other factors as well. Lupus can affect anyone, but women, as well as those of African American, Native American, Hispanic, and Asian descent, are more likely to develop the condition.

Neonatal and pediatric lupus erythematosus (NLE), discoid lupus erythematosus (DLE), drug-induced lupus (DIL), and systemic lupus erythematosus (SLE) are the four different types of lupus. The most typical form of lupus, known as systemic lupus erythematosus, impacts numerous bodily organs.

Cultivar lupus erythematosus, a skin condition that causes rashes and sores and is exacerbated by exposure to sunlight, is a condition that many lupus patients will develop. A physician may find it simpler to diagnose lupus in a patient if they have lesions, sores, or a rash.

An inflammation of the kidneys known as lupus nephritis, which can result in high blood pressure or kidney failure and require dialysis, may develop in some people. These symptoms include high blood pressure, blood in the urine, and swollen hands, ankles, or feet in lupus patients.

The presence of lupus cannot be determined by a single test.

A medical history review, physical examination, and questions regarding any autoimmune disease in the patient's family are all performed by doctors.

A skin or kidney biopsy, as well as a blood or urine test, might be necessary occasionally. You can find out if your immune system is producing lupus autoantibodies by taking an antinuclear antibody test (ANA).

Although there is no known treatment for lupus, symptoms and flare-ups can frequently be successfully managed with the right approaches. To stop lupus flare-ups and treat symptoms, doctors may prescribe immunosuppressants, corticosteroids, and antimalarial medications, to name a few. Depending on the patient, the type of lupus they have, and their particular response to treatment, a particular medication will be prescribed.

A well-rounded treatment program for lupus should include specific lifestyle changes. People with lupus can live healthier lives with fewer symptoms by quitting smoking, maintaining a healthy weight, eating well, and exercising frequently. Some people use natural and homemade remedies like MSM and turmeric to treat symptoms like pain and anxiety.

The best method for deciding on the best treatment strategy based on unique symptoms and needs is to speak with a healthcare professional.

Elroy Vojdani, MD, a functional practitioner certified by the Institute for Functional Medicine in Los Angeles, says that lupus is a very difficult autoimmune disease that needs a thorough treatment plan. "All patients should see a rheumatologist routinely and frequently who can help them navigate the appropriate medical options for managing or reducing the activity of this autoimmune disease; typical options include oral steroids, oral immunosuppressants, and oral/injectable biologics (medication that disables parts of the immune system). ".

Specialists in functional or integrative medicine may suggest additional treatments, such as a healthy diet, way of living, and supplements, that could help the overall condition.

TREATMENTS FOR LUPUS

Individual symptoms and drug responses will determine the kind of medication that is recommended to treat lupus. On a case-by-case basis, a healthcare professional can choose the appropriate medication, dosage, and form. A doctor may prescribe various medications, including immunosuppressants, corticosteroids, BLyS-specific inhibitors, and antimalarials. Medicines will be prescribed to manage flare-ups, balance hormones, lessen pain and swelling, and prevent joint damage.

Meds for malaria

Antimalarial medications have been shown to reduce the frequency and severity of lupus flare-ups as well as lengthen the lives of lupus patients. These two well-known antimalarial medications, Plaquenil (hydroxychloroquine) and Aralen (chloroquine phosphate), can relieve symptoms of joint pain, fatigue, and skin rashes. Stomach ache, nausea, vomiting, and diarrhea are typical antimalarial drug side effects.

particular inhibitors for BLyS.

These medications reduce the number of abnormal B cells that are present in lupus patients. An approved treatment for lupus is the BLyS-specific inhibitor Benlysta (belimumab). An allergic reaction, lightheadedness, and depression are typical side effects of this class of medication.

CORTICOSTEROIDS

Corticosteroids can aid in reducing lupus-related discomfort such as pain, swelling, and tenderness. High doses of corticosteroids are occasionally used to suppress the immune system, but they come with risks including depression, allergic reactions, and stomach pain. Dexamethasone Intensol and Solu-Cortef (hydrocortisone) are two corticosteroids that are frequently prescribed for lupus patients.

Prescription non-steroidal anti-inflammatory drugs

Nonsteroidal anti-inflammatory drugs (NSAIDs), such as ibuprofen and naproxen, are available over-the-counter and can be helpful for mild pain and swelling. These medications are available over the counter and are not intended to take the place of any prescription drugs for lupus that a doctor may issue.

Anti-cancer drugs and immune suppressants

Immunosuppressive drugs might be prescribed by a doctor to patients with severe organ-affecting lupus. These kinds of drugs are typically only used in severe conditions where other drugs have failed. They may have negative side effects that are severe and weaken the body's defenses against infection. An immunosuppressant used to treat lupus is Cellcept (mycophenolate mofetil).

Occasionally, lupus is treated with cancer drugs. They function by preventing the immune system from attacking healthy tissue and organs by stifling it. Cancer drugs include Rituxan (rituximab),

Cytoxan (cyclophosphamide), and Trexall (methotrexate). Risk factors for cancer medications may include brain infection, allergic reaction, and breathing difficulties.

Which drug treats lupus the best?

There isn't a single lupus treatment that works best for everyone. The way each person reacts to treatment and their symptoms varies. Based on a patient's symptoms, medical history, and response to treatments, a doctor can choose the most appropriate medication for treating lupus.

LUPUS: WHAT IS IT?

The immune system typically combats bacterial infections. When a person has lupus, their immune system malfunctions and instead of defending the body, it attacks healthy cells.

Nearly every organ in the body, including the blood vessels, joints, skin, kidneys, heart, lungs, and brain, is susceptible to lupus.

Lupus typically only affects a few areas of the body in most people and is a mild condition. While some patients do not experience inner organ issues, such as those affecting the heart and lungs, others may experience both skin and joint issues. Lupus typically has slow-moving symptoms that come and go. It may result in serious, potentially fatal issues for some people.

With proper care and management, a strong patient-provider relationship, and patients with illnesses that interfere with their organs' normal function, the prognosis is positive even for those patients.

The symptoms of lupus can vary from mild to severe in each individual and may appear and disappear over time.

THE PATHOGENESIS

When a person has lupus or another autoimmune disorder, their immune system is unable to distinguish between their own cells and tissues and foreign substances. The immune system then produces antibodies that attack the body, resulting in inflammation, pain, and organ damage.

A "flare," which happens when some symptoms appear for a brief time before going away, can occasionally be experienced by lupus sufferers. The patient can take action to deal with a flare by developing the ability to predict when one will occur. Many people experience extreme fatigue or aches, pains, rashes, fevers, stomachaches, headaches, or vertigo just before a flare.

DIAGNOSIS

Lupus cannot be diagnosed with a single test, and it may take months or years to do so. Lupus has no known cure, but certain medications and dietary adjustments can help control it.

HOW DOES LUPUS AFFECT PEOPLE?

Causes

There is no known cause of lupus. In most cases, the disease is brought on by a confluence of genetic, environmental, and possibly hormonal factors.

Although it does seem to run in families, lupus is not hereditary and no specific "lupus gene" has been found to date.

DESCRIBE LUPUS

Lupus is a chronic autoimmune disease that can result in pain and swelling all over your body. It is also known as systemic lupus erythematosus (SLE) or just lupus. The immune system of your body battles itself when you have an autoimmune disease. The immune system is intended to fight potential threats to the body, such as infections, but in this instance, it attacks healthy tissue.

In addition to joint pain, skin sensitivity and rashes, and problems with internal organs (the brain, lungs, kidneys, and heart), lupus patients may also experience rashes on their skin. There's a chance that many of your symptoms will flare-up frequently in waves. Lupus symptoms can occasionally be slight or undetectable (indicating remission).

Sometimes the condition's severe symptoms, which have a significant impact on your daily life, may manifest themselves.

What variations of lupus exist?

There are numerous varieties of lupus. The most typical type is systemic lupus erythematosus. Other forms of lupus include:.

Skin is affected by cutaneous lupus erythematosus, a type of lupus. Skin problems like rashes and sun sensitivity are common in people with cutaneous lupus erythematosus. Other symptoms of this condition include hair loss.

Drug-induced lupus: These lupus cases are brought on by specific medications. Though many of the symptoms of systemic lupus erythematosus may be present in drug-induced lupus patients, these symptoms are typically transient. Once the medication causing the lupus is stopped, it frequently disappears.

Neonatal lupus: This uncommon form of the disease affects newborn children.

Neonatal lupus patients have antibodies that were passed to them from their mother, who may have had lupus during her pregnancy or may develop the disease later in life. Not all children born to mothers who have lupus will go on to develop it.

How does lupus affect people?

Lupus can strike anyone. Women, men, kids, and even newborns can experience it. About 90% of diagnosed cases are women of reproductive age, making it much more common in women than in men. Because lupus is challenging to diagnose, experts have a hard time estimating how many Americans have the disease. Numerous symptoms of lupus can also be indicators of other illnesses. As a result, some lupus patients may live their entire lives without ever receiving a diagnosis.

Additionally, lupus is more prevalent in some ethnic groups. Asian, Native American, African-American, and Hispanic women are all more likely than Caucasian women to develop the condition.

If you have a family member who suffers from lupus or another autoimmune disease, your risk of developing the disease is also increased.

Do women tend to have lupus more often?

Nine out of ten cases of lupus occur in women, who also have a higher prevalence than men. Women are typically diagnosed between the ages of 15 and 44, which is during their fertile years. The hormone estrogen is thought to have some influence on lupus, despite the fact that the exact cause of the disease is unknown.

What changes the body does lupus make?

Numerous body parts may be affected by lupus. It may result in aches and pains as well as serious organ complications. Your body attacks itself when you have lupus because it is an autoimmune condition. Over time, this may result in organ damage.

The skin, blood, joints, kidneys, brain, heart, and lungs are just some of the body parts that lupus may affect.

Skin: Lupus often causes problems with the skin. Some lupus sufferers develop a red rash on their cheeks and the bridge of their nose. The name "lupus" (wolf in Latin) was given to this illness many years ago because the location of this rash corresponds with the typical wolf markings. Other skin issues include discoid lupus,which causes large, red, circular rashes (plaques) that may scar. Sunlight typically makes skin rashes worse. Additionally frequent are mouth sores and hair loss.

Blood: A blood involvement may occur with or without additional symptoms. The quantity of platelets (blood clotting cells), white blood cells, or red blood cells may dangerously decline in lupus patients. Changes in blood counts can occasionally contribute to symptoms of fatigue (low red blood cell count, anemia), serious infections (low white blood cell count), or easy bruising (low platelet count). It's crucial to have routine blood tests to check for any issues because many people do not exhibit symptoms that point to blood abnormalities. Blood clots occur more frequently in lupus patients. Deep venous thrombosis, also known as a lung clot, pulmonary embolism, and stroke are all common places for clots to form. Antiphospholipid antibodies may be linked to the development of blood clots in lupus patients. These antibodies are abnormal proteins that might make blood more likely to clot.

Joints: Lupus patients frequently have arthritis. With or without swelling, there may be pain. Mornings can be particularly painful and stiff. Arthritis can be a temporary issue that lasts a few days to weeks or it can be a chronic aspect of the illness. Fortunately, arthritis usually does not cause permanent disability.

Kidneys: Up to 50% of lupus patients may develop kidney involvement, which has a life-threatening potential.

Patients with lupus who experience joint pain, a rash, a fever, and weight loss may also have kidney problems.

Kidney disease can occasionally occur without any other lupus symptoms.

Typically, symptoms of kidney disease don't appear until it has advanced. Early detection and effective treatment of kidney disease are crucial. A urine test called a urinalysis can detect kidney disease at its earliest stages.

Brain: Thankfully, lupus sufferers rarely experience problems with brain involvement. Confusion, depression, seizures, and, incredibly, strokes may result from it when it's present.

Heart and lungs: Heart and lung involvement is frequently brought on by inflammation of the pericardium, which surrounds the heart, and the pleura, which covers the lungs. You may experience chest pain, an irregular heartbeat, and a buildup of fluid around the heart (pericarditis) and lungs (pleuritis or pleurisy) when these structures become inflamed.

SIGNIFICANCE AND CAUSES
What results in lupus?

Currently, it is unclear what causes lupus. To find out more about why lupus occurs, researchers are still doing research. There are elements that may contribute to the condition even though the precise cause is unknown. These are some of the potential causes of lupus.

Changes in hormones: Studies have shown that women are more likely than men to develop lupus, which may be at least partially attributed to hormones like estrogen. In women between the ages of 15 and 44, when estrogen levels are at their highest, lupus is frequently seen.

Environmental factors: Several elements of your environment may make you more likely to develop lupus. Lupus may be brought on by a variety of elements, including medications you take, viruses you may have been exposed to, stress, and how much sunlight you are exposed to. Lupus may also have a smoking history as a possible cause.

Your family's medical history: Lupus might be inherited.

Your risk of contracting lupus is raised if you have relatives who suffer from the condition.

What signs and symptoms do lupus have?

If you have lupus, there are many different symptoms you could encounter. There is no standard set of symptoms for lupus patients. Additionally, many of these symptoms are similar to those you might experience from other medical conditions. This is one of the difficulties in diagnosing someone with lupus.

Lupus symptoms might not appear right away.

Over time, you might experience new symptoms.

Your symptoms may also get progressively worse over time. Sometimes symptoms may barely be noticeable (in remission), while other times they may flare up. A flare-up occurs when a symptom becomes suddenly worse than it was.

Lupus signs and symptoms can consist of:.

- Joint pain.
- muscle ache.
- Rashes.
- Fever.

- sensitivity to light.
- Loss of hair.
- Mouth sores.
- wet eyes.
- Fatigue.

- Chest pain.

- Stomach pain.

- Shortness of breath.

- enlarged glands.

- Headaches.

- Confusion.

- Depression.

- Issues with the kidneys, heart or lungs.

- Seizures.

- Blood clots.

- Anemia.

- Raynaud's phenomenon.

What are the symptoms of lupus in women?

A majority of the people diagnosed with lupus are women. Women typically have lupus symptoms, but they can also develop complications that affect various body parts. These complications can include kidney problems (more commonly seen in African-American and Hispanic women than other groups), osteoporosis and heart disease.

What is the lupus rash?

A skin rash is one common symptom of lupus. Rashes from lupus are often from prolonged sun exposure, and usually last days to weeks. Your face, hands, or wrists may develop a rash. When you have a rash on your face, it typically extends across the bridge of your nose and onto each of your cheeks. This is often referred to as a "butterfly rash" because of the shape across your face.

Skin rashes can be uncomfortable and itchy. These rashes can sometimes fade after a short period of time. However, some rashes and sores on your skin can be permanent.

Why does lupus cause hair loss?
One of the complications of lupus can be damage to your skin and hair loss. People with lupus can develop scarring on their skin and scalp from rashes. Your hair may become brittle and thinning as a result. You could also experience hair loss

as a side effect of some medications that treat lupus — hair loss can be a side effect of steroids. Consult your healthcare provider if you notice that your hair is thinning or shedding. Sometimes, changing your medications can help with this issue. Your provider might also recommend using gentle shampoos (baby shampoo).

Why does lupus cause weight gain or weight loss?

Many people with lupus may experience weight loss. This can be caused by the medications that are used to treat lupus or from the discomfort of the disease itself. On the flip side, some people may gain weight if they find that they are inactive due to joint pain. It's important to maintain a healthy diet when you have lupus. Talk to your healthcare provider — and possibly a nutritionist (a food specialist) — to determine the best diet for you.

DIAGNOSIS AND TESTS

How is lupus diagnosed?

The diagnosis process can be long and difficult for lupus. The symptoms that you might experience with lupus can overlap with those of other conditions — for example, diabetes and arthritis. Symptoms of lupus may also take time to develop, adding to the challenge of diagnosing the disease.

Your healthcare provider will typically start with a family history to see if lupus runs in your family. Then, your provider will want to discuss any symptoms you've experienced. After talking to you about your symptoms, your provider will typically do some lab tests. These tests are looking for things like low blood cell counts, anemia and other abnormalities.

The provider may also do an antinuclear antibody (ANA) test. This test looks for antibodies — proteins in your body that defend against disease — that could be a sign you have an autoimmune disease. People who have systemic lupus erythematosus usually test positive for ANAs.

Does a positive antinuclear antibody (ANA) test mean I have lupus?

Testing positive for antinuclear antibodies alone does not mean you have lupus. The ANA test is positive in most people with lupus, but it's also positive in many people who do not have lupus. Because of this, a positive ANA alone isn't enough to diagnosis you with lupus. Your provider will typically look for at least three other clinical features (including symptoms and family history) before making a diagnosis of lupus.

MANAGEMENT AND TREATMENT

How is lupus treated?

- The way your provider treats lupus can depend on several factors, including:

- The symptoms and complications you are experiencing.

- The severity of your case.

- Your age.

- The type of medications you may be taking.

- Your general health.

- Your medical history.

Lupus is a life-long (chronic) condition that will needed to be managed regularly. The goal with treatment is to get your symptoms into remission (not active) and limit the amount of damage the disease does to your organs. Unfortunately, lupus can strike without warning, and its effects may change over time. You will need to regularly visit your healthcare provider and adapt your care plan to match your symptoms.

Some people with mild features of lupus might require limited treatment. These individuals may have symptoms that are monitored and watched to make sure they do not get worse, but they aren't currently in need of treatment. Others may need an aggressive treatment plan. These individuals tend to have more serious complications (like heart, lung or kidney complications). Your healthcare provider will discuss the best treatment options with you based on your symptoms, complications and medical history.

What are common lupus medications?

Lupus can be treated with the following medications:

Corticosteroids (including prednisone): Rashes can be treated with steroid creams directly. The use of creams is usually safe and effective, especially for mild rashes. The use of steroid creams or pills in low doses can be effective for mild or moderate features of lupus. Steroids can also be used in higher doses when internal organs are threatened.

Unfortunately, high doses are also most likely to produce side effects.

Hydroxychloroquine (Plaquenil): This medication is commonly used to help manage mild lupus-related problems, such as skin and joint disease. It's also used to treat fatigue and mouth sores.

Azathioprine (Imuran): A medication originally used to prevent rejection of transplanted organs, this is commonly used to treat the more serious features of lupus.

Methotrexate (Rheumatrex): This medication is another chemotherapy drug that's used to suppress the immune system. Its use is becoming increasingly popular for skin disease, arthritis and other non-life threatening forms of disease that have not responded to medications such as hydroxychloroquine or low doses of prednisone.

Cyclophosphamide (Cytoxan) and mycophenolatemofetil (CellCept): These medications are chemotherapy drugs that have very powerful effects on reducing the activity of the immune system. They are used to treat more severe forms of lupus, especially lupus that affects the kidneys.

Belimumab (Benlysta): This medication is a monoclonal antibody that reduces the activity of white blood cells (lymphocytes) that make autoantibodies. Autoantibodies are significant because they harm tissue. Belimumab is used to treat lupus that does not involve the kidneys and has not responded to other types of treatments.

Rituximab (Rituxan): A monoclonal antibody, this drug lessens the production of autoantibodies by white blood cells (lymphocytes). When other forms of treatment have failed to control lupus, it is occasionally used to treat it.

OUTLOOK OR FORECAST

Is it possible to treat lupus?

Lupus is currently incurable. Lupus treatment aims to control your symptoms and lessen the harm the condition causes to your body. Lupus will always be a part of your life, but it can be managed to lessen its effects.

Lupus has the potential to be fatal.

In most cases, organ damage and symptoms of lupus rather than the disease itself would be the cause of death. Heart disease, infections, and kidney damage are just a few of the conditions that can have fatal consequences.

Is lupus a communicable disease?

It is impossible to spread lupus from one person to another through touch, sneezing, or coughing.

125

If I have lupus, can I get pregnant?

Those who have lupus are capable of becoming pregnant.

However, lupus sufferers run the risk of having a miscarriage.

When scheduling a preconception appointment, start discussing your future pregnancy with your doctor several months in advance.

To make sure that your lupus medications are safe for pregnancy, your doctor may need to make a change.

Will I be able to pass on lupus to my kids if I have it?

Lupus may be influenced by genetics.

If you have relatives who suffer from the illness, your risk of developing lupus rises. Lupus can be transmitted from a mother to her child. However, it doesn't happen frequently or always in this way. Some lupus sufferers give birth to children who have the illness, while others do not. Consult your healthcare provider if you have lupus yourself or in your family and are considering becoming pregnant.

What can I do to stop lupus flare-ups?

While it is impossible to completely prevent lupus, there are things you can do to lessen the likelihood of symptom flare-ups. Among the things to try are:

Avoiding exposure to the sun: Sun exposure can be problematic for many lupus patients. By wearing protective clothing (long sleeves and a brimmed hat) and applying sunscreen, you can try to avoid going outside during the sun's peak hours.

Maintaining motion: Joint pain may tempt you to sit still and take it easy, but doing low-impact exercises can actually be beneficial.

Maintaining healthy routines: Some routines to remember include getting enough rest, limiting your stress levels, and making healthy food choices. Additionally, there is a direct correlation between lupus and heart disease. Make sure you are collaborating with your medical team to lower your risk of developing heart problems.

Treating lupus.

In order to safeguard your organs and stop flare-ups, your inflammation is the main focus of lupus treatment. A plan created for your unique requirements is the best method for treating your lupus. It ought to take into account the type of lupus you have, the degree of your inflammation, and the organ damage that has already taken place.

Remember that developing this plan may take some time, and it might need to be modified as your symptoms and your needs alter. Your treatment program's overarching objectives will be: in addition to system control.

Cut back on the inflammation.

Avoid flare-ups and deal with them as soon as they happen.lessen the amount of organ damage.

Talk to your doctor about the advantages, disadvantages, and side effects of any treatment you consider. Keeping track of your lupus and modifying your treatment as necessary requires regular exams and lab tests.

The Best Lupus Treatment Plan for You.

One or more of the following treatments may be suggested by your doctor:.

An effective antimalarial medication for lupus-related arthritis and rashes is hydroxychloroquine. It can help prevent blood clots and cuts down flares by 50%.

Immune suppressants and corticosteroids are frequently advised for people who have serious or life-threatening conditions like kidney inflammation, lupus, or lung, heart, or central nervous system disease. Prednisone and other high-dose corticosteroids fall under this category, as do medications that suppress the immune system like azathioprine,

131

cyclophosphamide, mycophenolate, and methotrexate.

Biologics: target specific immune system regions rather than the entire immune system as a whole. The FDA has given belimumab approval to treat lupus.

Alternative therapies for lupus-related complications.

Other medications may be recommended by your doctors to treat lupus-related issues.

Among them are:.

- seizures are treated with anticonvulsants.

- antibiotics are prescribed for infections.
- drugs that lower blood pressure, or antihypertensives.
- Statins are used to lower cholesterol.
- medications for osteoporosis.
- Vitamin D can help with kidney lupus.

Keeping Up a Healthy Lifestyle

The symptoms of lupus can be controlled by leading a healthy lifestyle. Here are a few simple steps you can take to look after yourself:.

- Consume a heart-healthy diet.
- Keep a healthy weight.

- Participate in regular exercise.
- Reduce your exposure to the sun by avoiding the sun as much as you can, covering up with clothing, and using SPF 100 sunscreen.
- For infections, consult a physician.
- Stop smoking.

What Impact Does Nutrition Have on Lupus?

Chronic inflammation is brought on by the autoimmune disease lupus. Due to an overactive immune system, people with lupus' bodies attack one another, which results in swelling and inflammation. The entire body is affected by this swelling. Fatigue, rashes, fever, and pain are possible side effects.

Organs may also be harmed by it.

Lupus symptoms come and go in episodes called flare-ups. Your physician might prescribe corticosteroids or anti-malarial medications to you during flare-ups to lessen inflammation. Making healthy lifestyle decisions may also lessen the frequency and intensity of flare-ups.

One way to manage your lupus is by eating healthy foods.

Lupus is affected by food
Doctors are discovering that diet has a significant impact on the reduction of inflammation. A 2019 study found that a low-calorie diet may slow the development of lupus. Also demonstrated to lessen fatigue is an anti-inflammatory diet.

Anti-inflammatory food

Natural ingredients found in anti-inflammatory foods help to reduce swelling. The following foods are anti-inflammatory:

- Berries, oranges, and tomatoes are examples of fruits.

- Green leafy vegetables like kale, spinach, and collard greens.

- Pecan and walnut nuts.

- Pomegranate juice, sweet potatoes, and berries are foods high in antioxidants.

- Salmon or tuna, flaxseed, and olive oil are foods high in omega-3 fatty acids.

- Flavonol-rich foods include watermelon, kiwis, apples, lentils, celery, broccoli, and asparagus.

Foods to stay away from

- Foodstuffs can exacerbate inflammation. These pro-inflammatory foods include, for instance:

- Saturated fat-rich foods include cheese and full-fat milk.

- beef is a red meat.

- sausage and hot dogs are processed meats.

- fried foods like chicken wings and french fries.

- processed foods like white bread and pastries.
- drinks, such as soda and sweetened beverages.

Risk of cardiovascular disease

Dietary control is crucial to maintaining a healthy weight. Your risk of heart issues increases if you are obese.

Given the elevated risk of heart disease already associated with lupus, this is particularly concerning.

Women with lupus who are ages 35 to 44 have a high risk of heart attacks. Their risk can be up to 50 times higher than that of women without lupus. The risk is 7 to 9 times higher for everyone with lupus compared to those without the disease.

Additional lupus-related health issues

Additionally, lupus sufferers have other health issues to consider. 7, 9, and 10 come to mind.

Half of lupus patients also have kidney problems, also known as lupus nephritis. Kidneys are harmed by lupus, which makes it difficult for them to filter waste.

Obesity-related health issues - Weight gain can be brought on by fatigue and steroid use. A lower quality of life, higher risk of cancer, diabetes, high blood pressure, heart issues, and depression are all associated with obesity.

139

Do not forget to talk to your doctor
Due to their elevated risk of heart issues, individuals with lupus frequently consume low-fat foods. Less protein may be necessary to protect the kidneys in lupus nephritis patients. If you use steroids, you might require a low-salt diet.

Based on your unique health profile, your doctor can assist you in modifying your diet.

The lupus medications you take may be affected by supplements and vitamins. Before ingesting any supplements, consult your doctor.

It can be overwhelming to alter your lifestyle. Introduce modifications one at a time. Don't forget to implement changes you can maintain. Key is consistency. Ask a licensed dietician for advice if you are unsure of where to begin. They can design a special diet for you based on your requirements. But before making dietary changes, be sure to consult your doctor.

There are five advantages to exercise for lupus management

Exercise is a crucial part of self-care, whether or not you have lupus.

Physical, emotional, and social advantages of exercise abound.

Since most lupus sufferers are able to engage in some form of activity, it is especially beneficial for them.

The following are some benefits of exercise for lupus management:

Exercise can strengthen your heart, lungs, bones, and joints, which may be impacted by lupus.

By controlling some of the chemical mediators of inflammation, exercise helps to reduce inflammation.

Exercise can keep your body in shape and help you manage weight gain brought on by corticosteroid use.

Your range of motion will increase with exercise, even if it's just light, low-impact movement, which will also help lower your risk of heart disease by reducing muscle stiffness.

Exercise may improve your mental health, making it simpler to handle life's stresses and possibly boosting your mood and self-esteem. Exercise can also lessen fatigue.

Working out with a friend can help you stay motivated to stick with your exercise program and turn your fitness time into social time if you're thinking about beginning an exercise program.

Make an effort to relax.

Lupus cannot be controlled by merely treating the physical symptoms. Stress reduction plays an important role in helping you live better with lupus.

Solutions for issues like exhaustion, pain, annoyance, and isolation.

Using exercise to build strength, flexibility, and endurance.

Best times to use their drugs.

Tips for communicating with family, friends, and their health care team.

Nutrition to support their health.

How to judge new treatments.

In comparison to women who only received a pamphlet, those who attended class reported significantly less stress after six weeks. There were lower self-reported rates of pain, fatigue, distress about one's health, limitations on social activities, and depression. These women continued to report lower depressive illness rates and higher well-being levels four months after the class.

Various methods for managing stress

There are two major categories for the different stress management techniques:.

Methods to manage pain, fatigue, and depression without the use of drugs or with fewer drugs.

Ways to streamline your life so you have less stress that may trigger flares or make managing flares more difficult.

No one stress management technique works for everyone. Before finding the right mix for you, you might need to try a few different approaches. Some of the most popular techniques used by lupus sufferers to lower stress are:.

- Relaxation.
- Exercise.
- Buddhist meditation and mindfulness.
- Biofeedback.
- Cognitive Behavioral Therapy.
- wholesome sleeping patterns

What is mindfulness and meditation?

Being mindful means being aware of your surroundings and your current feelings.

Meditation is very similar to mindfulness. With meditation, you focus on a certain thought or object to clear your mind and calm your emotions. It is easy to stop noticing the world around you or your own emotions. Stopping to notice a pretty fall leaf or a child's laughter can bring you joy. Learning to tap into your feeling helps you understand yourself better, which can help you manage stress.

How does biofeedback work?
You can learn the method of biofeedback and use it to regulate some bodily processes. Taking slow, deep breaths to relax or lower your heart rate is a straightforward illustration. It takes practice and training to master more complex biofeedback techniques.

Numerous physical and psychological problems, including pain, headaches, anxiety, and high blood pressure, can be treated with biofeedback. It occasionally aids individuals in lessening their dependence on drugs.

The cognitive behavioral therapy: what is it?

A brief form of therapy called cognitive behavioral therapy (CBT) focuses on solving problems practically. A person is encouraged by CBT to comprehend and alter their way of thinking about problems in order to improve their life. An illustration would be to consider your abilities rather than the limitations of your lupus.

To prevent wasting too much energy, practice saying no.

- Sort out your priorities, then start with the most crucial tasks.
- Request assistance at home and modifications at the office.
- For important activities, plan ahead.

- Negative self-talk should be replaced with supportive, uplifting ideas.
- Make time in your schedule for sleep.
- Regular exercise is advised.
- Become a member of a lupus support group.
- Volunteer if you're lonely.

Nobody is able to completely eliminate the stress in their lives. However, you can find ways to lessen some of it and cope with life's ups and downs better.

Many lupus sufferers claim that times of stress trigger flare-ups. It makes no difference whether a significant event like a divorce or minor everyday hassles are to blame for this stress. You aid yourself in minimizing pain and other potential symptoms by learning to maintain calm or avoid stress.

Lupus: Signs, Diagnosis, and Treatment

A long-lasting autoimmune condition is lupus. Its wide range of symptoms, which frequently resemble those of other illnesses, make it challenging to diagnose. This makes it even more crucial for people who experience any unusual symptoms to get the appropriate lupus testing and evaluation from medical professionals.

This thorough guide will cover everything you need to know about lupus testing, including the various types of tests that are available and what they measure. For vital information on getting tested and accurately diagnosed, keep reading if you or someone you know has lupus or thinks they might.

What precisely is lupus?

An autoimmune condition is lupus. Any area of the body may be harmed. The heart, brain, and lungs can occasionally be affected by lupus.

The condition cannot be identified through lupus testing. To reach a diagnosis, doctors frequently combine several tests. The most typical tests for lupus include:.

Blood Tests: Blood tests are a crucial component of the lupus testing process. Levels of inflammation and lupus antibodies can be measured with tests like Lupus Anticoagulants (LAC) profiles.

Urinalysis: In this lupus test, kidney damage is looked for. Lupus often causes kidney damage.

Imaging tests: These can aid in the search for indications of organ deterioration or inflammation. X-rays, ultrasounds, and MRIs are frequently used imaging tests to identify lupus.

Erythrocyte Sedimentation Rate: In this test, the rate at which red blood cells sink to the bottom of a test tube is gauged.

Increased rates suggest that the body is inflamed.

Assessment of the Liver and Kidneys: These tests can also help identify whether lupus is causing damage to the liver or kidneys.

Test for antinuclear antibodies (ANA): This procedure can help identify antibodies that are produced when the immune system of the body is attacking its own cells. While the majority of those with lupus have positive ANA results, the majority of those with positive ANA results do not have lupus. Your doctor might suggest more focused antibody testing if you test positive for ANA.

Lupus can cause a wide range of symptoms. They can differ from person to person. While some lupus sufferers may only experience a few mild symptoms, others may experience more severe ones.

Fatigue is the most typical sign of lupus. It may be difficult to perform daily tasks due to this symptom, which can be very debilitating. Other typical signs include stiffness and pain in the joints, skin rashes, hair loss, and kidney issues.

You must visit your doctor for a diagnosis if you are exhibiting any of these signs, and they will suggest lupus testing.

Therapy for lupus

There is no one-size-fits-all lupus treatment. This is due to the fact that each individual's condition can vary greatly. Taking into account the outcomes of the Lupus test, treatment plans are frequently created on a case-by-case basis.

Nevertheless, common medical procedures are frequently used to manage lupus. These consist of:.

Anti-inflammatory medications: These can aid in lowering body-wide inflammation. Corticosteroids (like prednisone) and nonsteroidal anti-inflammatory drugs (NSAIDs), like ibuprofen or naproxen, are frequent examples.

Drugs that suppress the immune system: These medicines work to reduce the immune response of the body. This may lessen inflammation and stop flare-ups. Azathioprine, cyclophosphamide, and methotrexate are examples of common immunosuppressive medications used to treat lupus.

Antimalarial medications: These drugs are frequently used to treat malaria, but they can also aid in the treatment of lupus. They function by assisting in the management of inflammation and curbing flare-ups. Chloroquine and hydroxychloroquine are typical antimalarial medications used to treat lupus.

157

Biologic agents are a more recent class of medication. They assist in concentrating on particular immune system organs. They can be helpful in treating severe lupus cases that haven't responded to conventional therapies. Rituximab and belimumab are common biologic medications used to treat lupus.

Changing your way of life can help you manage your lupus symptoms and prevent flare-ups. This could entail engaging in regular exercise, eating a balanced diet, lowering your stress level, and getting adequate rest.

Massage, acupuncture, yoga, and meditation are examples of complementary therapies that can help people relax and reduce stress. This can aid in lupus symptom management.

Corticosteroids: Corticosteroids are potent anti-inflammatory medications. They can be applied to lessen pain, swelling, and inflammation. They are typically ingested or injected directly into the area that is affected. Utilizing corticosteroids for a brief period of time can be helpful in treating lupus flares. Long-term use, however, may result in serious side effects like weight gain, bone thinning, high blood pressure, and an increased risk of infection.

residing with lupus.

Although there is no known cure for lupus, there are treatments that can help manage symptoms and lessen flare-ups. Consult your physician frequently for checkups and to track your symptoms if you have lupus. In order to control the disease, you might also need to take medication.

Lupus can make daily life difficult, but there are ways to manage the condition. For the best symptom management, it's critical to stay informed about your condition and work closely with your doctor. To assist you in coping with lupus, there are support groups and other resources available.

The doctor may advise routine lupus testing to keep track of medication effects or gauge how well symptoms are being controlled. In such circumstances, it is the patient and caregiver's responsibility to ensure that all prescribed tests are completed and the results are given to the doctor for an assessment.

What to Eat and Avoid on the Best Lupus Diet.

The skin, joints, and internal organs are most frequently affected by the chronic autoimmune disease lupus, which also results in widespread inflammation and pain. Lupus begins as an immune system malfunction, like other autoimmune diseases. It attacks healthy tissue rather than defending itself against disease and infection as it should. While there are numerous treatment options that can help with lupus symptoms, lifestyle decisions, like your diet, can have a significant impact on how the disease affects your body. However, what foods should lupus sufferers avoid eating and what diet is best for them?

Dietary Guidelines for Lupus.

For those who have lupus, there is no magic diet. To reduce inflammation and flare-ups, a healthy diet and lifestyle are far preferable. Considering this, certain foods may offer lupus sufferers additional advantages.

Lupus patients are more likely to experience bone diseases like osteoporosis and osteopenia. Foods high in calcium can aid in your defense against some of these ailments. Calcium-rich foods include the following:

- dark greens with many leaves.
- Beans.
- Antioxidant-rich foods.

Vitamin A, Vitamin B, and Vitamin E are antioxidants that can help prevent inflammation and other kinds of cell damage. Some lupus sufferers discover that foods high in antioxidants can help prevent flare-ups, though the exact benefits for these patients are still unknown. include among these foods.

- Fruits.
- Vegetables.
- legumes and nuts.

- Granola and oats.

- the teas black and green.

- Foods to Steer Clear Of.

Certain foods contain ingredients that naturally strengthen immunity. While this might be advantageous for someone with a strong immune system, it can trigger flare-ups and cause inflammation in someone with lupus. Do not forget that lupus is an autoimmune disease, which means that the body's immune system attacks itself. Therefore, anything that boosts the immune system comes with an inherent risk of making an autoimmune disease like lupus worse. Avoiding certain common foods includes:.

ALFALFA.

L-canavanine, an amino acid found in alfalfa and alfalfa sprouts, is immune system-stimulating.

It is best to stay away from anything that contains alfalfa.

Garlic.

White blood cells, which typically aid the body in fighting disease, can be increased thanks to substances in garlic like allicin, ajoene, and thiosulfinates. The immune system being stimulated, however, can cause flare-ups in lupus patients. Garlic should be avoided whenever possible even though small amounts may not be harmful.

Saturated fat and cholesterol-rich foods.

Patients with lupus should be especially watchful of foods with known links to heart disease, such as red meat, fried foods, and dairy, as their risk of heart attack is 50 times higher.

Echinacea.

The immune system booster echinacea is frequently found in supplements designed to strengthen your defenses against the common cold and other seasonal illnesses. Such an increase in energy is harmful for people with autoimmune diseases, just like the other foods on this list. Consult your doctor and ensure that any supplements you take are free of echinacea by reading the labels.

www.ingramcontent.com/pod-product-compliance
Lightning Source LLC
Chambersburg PA
CBHW070934260726
48661CB00003B/982